Cholo✦Style

Homies, Homegirls & La Raza

REYNALDO BERRIOS
and *MI VIDA LOCA* Magazine

FERAL HOUSE

Feral House
PO Box 39910
Los Angeles, CA 90039

www.feralhouse.com
10-digit ISBN: 1-932595-14-7
13-digit ISBN: 978-1-932595-14-7

10 9 8 7 6 5 4 3 2 1

Design by Dana Collins

The Publisher wishes to thank Christina (Ween) Chokas
and Jason Louv for their editorial assistance.

To contact Reynaldo Berrios
and *Mi Vida Loca* Magazine:
P.O. Box 423567
San Francisco, CA 94142

CONTENTS

FOREWORD
REYNALDO BERRIOS ON
CHOLO STYLE AND
MI VIDA LOCA MAGAZINE

The Cholo 'zine *Mi Vida Loca* was straight from the street. Amazing vernacular illustrations of teary and laughing homicidal clowns drawn by prisoners from Folsom, Soledad, Pelican Bay, Corcoran and Victor A. Spider ... pen pal solicitations from lonely chicas... interviews with and snapshots of gang sets throughout the state... fervent exhortations to La Raza and Aztlan... even directives from some original gangster about the proper manly way to take care of a dispute: "No Drive-Bys!"

I knew that the material would make a remarkable book, a snapshot of a time and place and style that has great influence in our culture today. So I called its editor, and we agreed to meet at a bar in San Francisco's Mission District.

The bar was quite the dingy watering hole, and I didn't know who I was looking for, but out of a dark corner came Reynaldo Berrios, who was already nursing a whisky.

After we shook hands, the first thing he did was motion me over to the back door, where some light was shining through a nearby shattered window. Then he unbuttoned a flannel shirt and moved his stocky chest into the light. Scars, knife scars, crisscrossed his chest and stomach like angry, confused train tracks.

"Hey man, I want you to know this is no bullshit, this is the real thing."

I never doubted this claim, even before I met Rey Berrios. After another drink or two we sat down and talked. The first thing I asked him about was the war between Southern and Northern California "Gangsters." Reading *Mi Vida Loca*, I knew that some guys he grew up with in the San Francisco area later moved down to Logan Heights in San Diego.

– Adam Parfrey

VICTOR A. SPIDER & REYNALDO BERRIOS OF *MI VIDA LOCA* MAGAZINE

AP: *What did those friends tell you when you visited San Diego?*
REY: The first thing they told me when I got off the Greyhound bus was "Reynaldo, don't tell them you are from San Francisco. If you do, you gonna get fucked up and we gonna get fucked up for bringing a vato from Norte Califas to Diego. Tell everyone that you are from East L.A. Anyways, you look like an LA vato." So I said, "What the fuck, I ain't no chavala, if they want to fight I'll fight them!" Then they said, "How about us, you are just visiting while we live here, and we could get killed."

One night, we went to a park and a lot of Logan Heights homeboys were there, then two vatos came up to me and asked in a friendly manner where I was from. I said, "East Los." Then their eyes lit up and they asked how was it in East Los. I felt like a coward and quickly I responded, "I ain't from no fucking East Los, I'm from San Fran. The Mission District. You know the Golden Gate Bridge, where they have that fake pyramid building."

Then I got ready to fight, ready for the desmadre! But to my amazement they kept their eyes all lit up and asked, "How is it out there, homes?" Right away I knew I'd met some friendly faces, and then I explained to them how the Mission District is the place to cruise bumper-to-bumper and that girls come from all over to party with San Franeros.

What did your friends say?
Their reaction was, "Fucking Reynaldo, you don't give a fuck." They knew that sooner or later I was going to tell their homies where I'm from regardless of the situation. Later, we were all fighting against vatos from National City. And, at some Logan Heights party, a guy about our age who had big pull with the carnales wanted to jump me, but my homies backed me up. That's true friendship right there. Rest in peace Zorro de Logan Heights, San Diego Sur Califas.

How has getting people together regardless of barrio gone?

Getting homeboys together from different barrios or from different geographical areas within Califas for the sake of Aztlan has been impossible for me—but I have had secret meetings with different individuals who are at war, to iron out personal differences! Solid homeboys trust me 'cause I take no sides, for I follow La Raza's traditional ways of doing things. I live and will die in that style.

Explain Aztlan a little bit.

Aztlan is where our ancestors emerged from, which is someplace in the southwestern part of the United States. God gave us life in Aztlan and sent down a messenger to tell us to leave it and travel to the four corners of our bronze continent and to come back to Aztlan. Aztlan is our motherland and our birthright! Ain't no fucking transplanted European gonna keep us away from our birthright! We are coming back, baby!

California is the base of the whole Aztlan world, then?

I don't know about California being a base, but from what I've seen through my travels, we are all over! The southern part of California is where the most outspoken people in defending our rights are. Tejas is too laid back. In Nuevo Mexico there are too many sellouts! In Arizona, two Hopi friends of mine took me to a kiva from which our ancestors emerged. The whole place is sacred but all the clans and different tribes must protect it from the whites!

The race started there in Arizona?

As I said, I was taken to a sacred place where my ancestors emerged from and it's some place in Arizona. White people are not allowed there! And it's a secret and sacred place. I can't say any more than that!

Aren't you part Spanish, part European, part white?

We are mestizos. We have the noble bloodline of the Mayas, Aztecas, Apaches, Incas, Toltecas and hundreds of other tribes, plus the blood of Spanish conquistadores. Both the indigenous people and the Spaniards refused to accept each other's worlds, and so they fought to the death! Warriors against conquistadores! Many indigenous tribes survived and have preserved their culture. I have seen them and they don't trust the whites! Mestizos have kept some culture alive while blending in with some Spaniard beliefs. But our bloodline is indigenous to America, indigenous to Aztlan. The first mestizos were products of Spaniard conquistadores raping young indigenous girls throughout America. Both Spaniards and indigenous people saw mestizos as garbage. But later we gained our respect by fighting side-by-side with our indigenous brothers and sisters against European invaders. We've been fighting them for more than 500 years.

Is that a fight in your own system, then?

Since I'm here in America and not in Europe, I am indigenous! My heart and soul belong to my indigenous ancestors. There's been a lot of European invasion here in America, not just by the Spanish conquistadores but also by the French, English, Portuguese, Germans and many others.

REYNALDO
BERRIOS AND
VICTOR "SPIDER"
AVENA, BERNAL
HEIGHTS, SAN
FRANCISCO

Some of our people carry a bit of that Euro blood, but it does not affect us, 'cause our indigenous bloodline and culture supersedes everything else! This is foreign to a white American, 'cause he has no culture! A white man's culture in the U.S. is hot dogs, cheeseburgers, SUVs. Shit, we have SUVs and we eat hot dogs and cheeseburgers, but we have retained our values, morals and culture!

Didn't La Raza have a bigger movement in the '60s than today?
Yes, today we are sound asleep, while white America spits in our faces and calls us illegal aliens. Back in the '60s, we were forming our own political movement. There were Brown Berets, César Chávez was defending farm workers, and Latino/Chicano students were demanding our rights as native people of Aztlan.

How do you feel about the use of Chicanos by corporate culture, for the sake of advertising?
The Chicanos that are in the middle, they're a bit whitewashed. People like me who've got a lot of pride and a lot of culture, we don't buy the sales pitch 'cause we don't identify with it.

Then your sense of La Raza culture is not the same as what corporate entities are trying to put over as La Raza culture?
Correct. Those idiots are missing out on how to reach into our pockets. Our money goes out to those that give us some respect.

How do you tell the difference between bullshit and true culture?
True culture happens within families, with friends, at parties. It comes with a gathering of students brainstorming plans to better our barrios, celebrate our past and honor our heroes. Showing some fake Latinos dancing to some music just don't cut it with us!

ILLUSTRATION BY
VICTOR A. SPIDER

Mi Vida Loca Magazine

You know where I go to buy my style of music, which is La Raza type of music—I have to come down to L.A., to go to Sounds of Music or to Musica Latina in the Mission District and find out what type of CDs are out there that are made by some straight-up homies. Or pick up some good cumbias, banda or corridos. I don't listen to the garbage they put out these days, 'cause I can't relate to it.

La Raza is not Jennifer Lopez then.
No, of course not. You know what, Jennifer Lopez to us is like another white woman. She's not one of us. All the homies were mad when she put blacks on low rider bikes; why couldn't she use little cholitos? She's a fucking sellout. Low riding is our onda!

Is hip-hop overruling La Raza culture? Is there such a thing as authentic La Raza hip-hop?
There is some straight-up Chicano hip-hop, that relates to our style out there, but it's not being put on the mainstream radio stations. So they sell it underground. See, the blacks and the whites are getting married, and they're the ones who control the music industry, and they do not want to see our people come up.

Why is that?
The white boys and black boys have some kind of relationship, and they want kids to either listen to the fucking freaking white boys or the fucking freaking black boys. I say fuck both of them and let's stop buying their CDs. Right now I'm traveling, going to the barrios' frontlines to recruit Chicano rappers and see what we can do to expose our kind of music to Aztlan and the rest of the world!

We hear more and more about Middle America filling up with Chicanos…

This is what's happening in the big cities. There are technological and biotech companies, along with other big industries, coming into the big cities like San Francisco, San Jose, Los Angeles and San Diego, and moving Latinos and Chicanos out. The gang task forces make up any type of bullshit to give Chicanos false charges and send them to the can. Schools in the barrios have very little money coming in, so they need supplies, and rent goes up. Real estate people put big pressure on Latino homeowners to sell. And you also get redistricting laws to move La Raza out. I was in San Diego about a month ago. As soon as I reached Logan Heights, in less than ten minutes three police cars were following me. Where the fuck do we live? The old Soviet Union, or what? What the police and city government are doing is chasing the Chicanos out, bringing in the white people and giving the blacks Section 8. Sooner or later chasing us out will backfire on white people. So now we are going to Middle America.

Is this move a work thing?

Latinos, Chicanos, we don't give a fuck, man! We'll work. Anything that comes up, we'll work. You know what I mean?

Why do you think that is?

It's because we have a sense of obligation to the family. We have a sense of pride. We don't want shit to be given to us, and we don't want to beg for anything. We want to work for what we have. Whatever we have to do, we'll work for it, in every sense of the word.

What inspired you to start* Mi Vida Loca *magazine in 1992?

There were hundreds of reasons. Mostly we were being ignored. Mainstream people ignore us—we're in our own land, and there's millions of us, and when you turn on the TV you only see white and black faces, you never see a brown face. That pisses me off. I don't know why the rest of our people don't get pissed off; we're supposed to live in a democratic society, and yet our voices are not being heard. What the fuck is going on? When I see some white TV show or black TV show, I can't relate to that, because that's not me, so I turn the shit off. Then I wanted to unite the homeboys, stop drivebys, and fight for our rights. I wanted to promote education, push Latinas and Chicanos to go on to college. I wanted my race to start helping each other out instead of trying to kill one another. And I wanted my people to have a voice in the magazine to express their hurt, anger, sorrow, joy, creativity and pride.

When you were able to vocalize things, did you start to feel that things were getting better?

It's getting worse and worse. It's like we don't exist. We continue to be the unheard masses. We are at the bottom of the barrel when it comes to political representation, economical progress and social status. Right now we have hateful politicians screaming that my

ARTE BY
TONITO B.
DE SAN PEDRO,
HARBOR AREA

beloved people are illegal aliens. Now, let me remind those hateful white people that we are in our own land and if they don't like our proud, beautiful faces then go back to Europe and leave us natives alone! As for cowards doing drive-bys, it has slowed down a lot but there are a few loose screws thinking that such cowardly acts will gain them a medal. In the first place, innocent kids and mothers get the bullet; in the second place, your rival has already spotted you; and in the third place, there are one too many witnesses. So you are fucked either way. And most important, cara a cara is our way of handling this stuff.

It's cowardly to do that drive-by shit, huh?
Yeah. Damn right! We didn't grow up that way. I didn't grow up that way. I grew up like, hey, if you've got a problem with somebody, you go right up to his fucking face and say "Hey ese, me and you, we've got to settle it a putasos!"

But you're not really for that bullshit fighting, vato vs. vato?
No, listen, there's always going to be problems, right? And if you can't talk it over, if you can't solve it by talking the problems over, then fuck it. Just box it out. It'll be between you and that person and nobody else. And if you're too fucking hardheaded to understand, box and box until one day, you know what, you're gonna see that guy, he's gonna respect you. You fought him so many times, you both are going to respect each other so much, that one day you're going to tell that dude, "Hey holmes, you want a beer?" He'll say yeah. And right there and then you'll iron out your differences. And when you're doing drive-bys, you're not talking. You're just creating hate!

***Your magazine. It's against the drive-bys. It's for the culture.
Any other motivating reasons? Like Reynaldo Berrios wanting
to tell his own story?***

I started writing about my life in the magazine, and it was called
"Life in the Barrio, Soy Como Soy." My whole life has been one motion picture after another and *MVL* fans ate it up. They wanted more
and more of Beto, which is my pen name in the story. So I gave them
their monthly soap opera, which was all real, but I left out people's
names to protect their identities.

***A lot of La Raza are ignorant of the past now. Do you think
there's a conspiracy to keep them ignorant?***

There's an old saying that goes something like this: "If you don't
know where you came from, you won't know where you are going."
And it's true for younger and older Chicanos that don't know our
rich and proud history. They let gringos walk all over them, and they
let gringos take away their rights not only as human beings but their
rights as natives of America. We have been treated as foreigners in
our America for too long.

***You did* Mi Vida Loca *for nine years and more than 70 issues.
That's a long time and a lot of magazines. Do you feel that you
built something?***

As an individual, walking the streets on the front lines, I had my face
and back in front of guns one too many times. But my balls and sincerity kept me from getting a bullet in my head. And, of course, my
guardian angels. I found brotherhood among those that will kill you
in a second if you are a traitor or a coward. To those blood brothers
I'm their carnalito, their little brother. They worried about me when
I went out into new territory, 'cause they knew of all the dangers I
would confront, but I survived each journey. Even when I lost, I still
won. Because no one else had the courage and love for all the barrios in Aztlan that I did. None of it was a waste of time 'cause I still
have those solid bonds, and I help out a lot of misguided cholitas
and cholitos.

***Let's say it's the best of all possible worlds for you, with Aztlan
once again in charge of its own land. Have you thought about
what happens then?***

That has been prophesied. Cause we *are* in our own land! Elders
from different tribes will get together and form a just government
for everyone. Different points of view will be presented and all will
be considered, and only those points of view that will include the
whole nuclear family will be considered.

What do you mean by nuclear family?

Since we have bloodlines from Africa, Asia and Europe living among
us Mestizos and indigenous in our continent, we will include you
guys as well, for we all came from the Omnipotente, the Creator of
Heaven and Earth, and if we are to live in harmony and happiness,
blacks, whites and Asians will be part of the whole family. ৵

VICTOR A. SPIDER AND
REYNALDO BERRIOS

1.

INTRODUCTION

"Carnalito, you have stopped being a part of what was not only holding you down, but what perpetuated the nothingness that gang warfare is about. That itself is a big deal. Now you've elevated yourself to a point where you're building your own mind, so that you'll have the knowledge it takes to do something, and with the magazine, you're doing something firme. You're well on your way to finding a way, Rey, and I have no doubt that you will make your mark; I'm sure of it. When you educate our people on how and why they are where they are right now, the gavachos call it reverse racism. You can't speak of the past acts and atrocities against our gente without people calling it hate. In attempting to wake up the sleeping giant, you automatically send an invitation to those in power. They've spent hundreds of years sedating us, and if you come close, you will be put on cross after cross. But you already know that, ese. When you are spinning your wheel, all eyes will be on you! You have a long hard journey in which your testicles will be put to the test. Those close to you will stab you in the back. People will be jealous of you. Others will hate you, and when the shit hits the fan, you will be alone! I know you, you will overcome all the pitfalls and obstacles on your journey, 'cause your heart pumps the blood of a warrior. You are earning your respeto the hard way, from the front lines! When you plan on reaching long and wide, you must cater to both north and south equally. Siempre, tu carnal."

Ovo. My name is Reynaldo Berrios. I am the creator of *Mi Vida Loca* magazine. Over the last nine years, we have put out 77 issues. My homeboy, Victor A. Spider, el artista de *Mi Vida Loca* magazine, does the artwork for the front covers. Victor has been a firme homie with a good heart. Now, as for the libro, I'm not going to beat around the bush in making my point. I'm going to be direct. I know that some people will not like that, because they are weak or greedy. In contrast, I know that my libro will do the following: It will remove the blinders from the little homeboys and homegirls throughout Aztlan and encourage them to become productive members of the Chicano/Latino communities. The Latinas and Chicanos that act and talk like the blacks and whites will get their feelings hurt, while the Asian-Americans, European-Americans, African-Americans and Arabic-Americans will be educated on the real "Americans," the Indio-Hispano race, my gente, my bloodline! La sangre de los Nicoyas, Aztecas, Mayans, Incas, Toltecas, Apaches, Hopis and hundreds more. In addition, I'm going to take you on a journey to a place where my life was at stake one too many times, but due to my cora, sincerity and (to put it bluntly, you have to be a fucking nut) pues, I kept myself from getting killed—and I never sacrificed my honor! I stuck to my objectives and went toe-to-toe with the consequences. I will personally take you into some of those dark moments when my life was at stake, and I will also share with you the carnalismo that I encountered and the love that my gente gave me because of my work.

As a carnalito and as a "little brother," there are certain behind-the-scenes turicas I can't disclose due to trust and carino among solidos. I know for a fact that this libro will bring out the goodness of all people, 'cause it has been written with a lot of huevos y mucho carino! I want my gente, the Nicaragueneses, Chicanos, Guatemaltecos, Salvadorenos, Costa Ricenses, Peruanos, Colombianos, Mexicanos, Hondurenos and más to embrace our cultura and keep our cultura alive! For individuals to work for their betterment and help out their familias so we can become strong voice in the political arena, become economically stable, and socially clean up our own mierda and push our gente forward! Point of clarification: Stop the chismes (que parecen putas del mercado). We tend to pull each other down the ladder instead of pulling each other up the charco de mierda that we have created for ourselves. Me entienden!

To all of you Asian, black and white people that have picked up this firme libro, I will share with you the loneliness, the pain, the confusion, the illusions, the hope, the pride, the carino and the carnalismo of my race, the Indio-Hispanic race. These are the másses you see every day of the week and ignore. Pues guess what, you can't fucking ignore us anymore! We keep on multiplying, and we keep on consuming. Some businesses cannot, and will not, survive without our purchasing power—so you better treat us with some respect and count us into your profits. Start giving back to our communities! All you European-Americans, whose ancestors stole the land of my ancestors, remember where you came from! In the process of your

invasion, we fought you and killed you as well. And as for all you African Americans, we get tired of your bitching and crying over slavery. Shit! Every race on this Earth has been a slave at one time or another. And proudly I tell you this, no pinche Abe Lincoln gave my people our freedom! We fought for it over and over again. The whites killed us and we killed them! Deep down in their cowardly hearts they fear the "Brown-n-Proud." That's why they use us against each other in every way imaginable. It's fucking sad, hey, but true.

To all the high school and middle school teachers throughout Aztlan, my deepest and sincerest respect to each and every one of you. You have an honorable and respectable job encouraging kids to have goals and dreams. If I had the political power of increasing your salary and decreasing your classroom size, I would. Many times you will have a youngster acting out as if they were a hardcore gang member, or some will isolate themselves and be real quiet and hardly show up for class. Please don't give up on them, 'cause everybody else has. My counselor, my principal and a few of my teachers gave up on me, but guess what—I eventually graduated, went on to a university and I proudly taught living skills, U.S. history and geography to high school students. Then I went on to teach language arts and world history to middle school kids. So don't give up on them, 'cause I didn't. Brown, yellow, white, black—they were all my students at one time or another.

Now open yourself up to my world... but before I begin, let's give everybody a consejo. No matter how fucked up your life is right now, trust yourself and rebuild your confidence. Put everybody aside, set your objective and goal, and go for it full blast. Don't let anything hold you back.

My life has been a series of stages: the baby stage, the li'l chavalito stage, the pre-teen stage and the teenager stage. I got stuck in the teenage stage well over my years. This was due to my "I don't give a fuck" attitude and my "I'm indestructible" attitude. Sadly, some people never get out of this stage, while some live it short and then go on with their manhood or womanhood. Unfortunately, many of us that grow up in the barrio get stuck in that stage and never venture into the world. Due to today's technology, the world is getting smaller and we must go out into the world and learn of the many resources out there so we can live a better life. I'm going to share with you a small part of my life. It's called, "Life in the Barrio, Soy Como Soy."

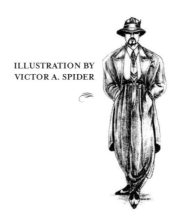

2.

LIFE IN THE BARRIO,
SOY COMO SOY

Before I tell you people about myself, I need to tell you about my ancestors. The creator gave us life and commanded my ancestors to walk to the four corners of our bronze continent and come back to our place of birth, someplace in Arizona known as Aztlan. We had to do this so we could purify ourselves from previous sins caused by people from the fourth world. Upon leaving Aztlan, someplace in Arizona, prophets told my ancestors to move south until they found a large body of water with two mountains rising from the center. So they walked from what is known today as Arizona to Central America at the shores of Lago de Nicaragua long ago, like the Miskitos and Samu of Colombian descent. Also the Chorotegas of Aztec descent and the Chontales of Maya descent. We all came from Aztlan! I am a true native of "America," I did not cross an ocean to get here, I've been here since the beginning of time. My soul and blood are of indigenous roots, but my languages are both European, those of Spain and England. Nicaragueneses have fought against themselves and against other indigenous nations as well as the English, Spaniards and other European nations. My people even fought against the U.S. Marines because the United Fruit Company and U.S. corrupted officials wanted Nicaragua to be a banana republic while they controlled its resources and people. But General Sandino fought against U.S. invaders with stones and machetes in the jungles and defeated the U.S. Marines. I take a lot of pride in my people for fighting against all odds for our liberty, our land and the pursuit of happiness.

My bloodline is of warrior and revolutionary descent as well as of artistic, scientific and herbalist skill, with a deep-rooted connection with Mother Earth. As a kid growing up, I was taught to have respect for myself and for others, especially my elders and the handicapped. I grew up with morals and values. I was the type of kid that

ARTE BY FRANK. A,
SOUTHLAND

would get up and give my seat to a senior citizen, a lady carrying her groceries, or anyone carrying a baby. But we live in a society where not everyone is taught to have respect, and when I got disrespected, my warrior and revolutionary blood came out in full force.

I believe that all of us men—whether you are Indio-Hispanic, Chicano, Asian, black or white that grew up in the barrio or ghetto—have growing stages in life, and we often get stuck in the teenage stage for years and years. We don't let go and get over our juvenile ways, and we don't invest in re-educating ourselves for our own growth. I don't mean to say to become pinche square! Chale! We need to catch up with the ever-changing world or be left behind fighting over pennies and nickels and become cattle for the money-making prison cartels and corrupt officials. For years I got stuck in my teenage stage and slowed down my growth as a responsible man of the world. For years I've been thinking like a teenager, and it's embarrassing saying this, but I say it so that I can help someone else get out of that stage: Move on to a responsible manhood stage and take care of your loved ones.

I was born in San Francisco, California to Nicaraguenese parents. At the age of two, my father came rushing home one night and told my mom to pack everything and go, 'cause he had just bashed a frying pan on his boss' head, leaving him on the floor. His boss was a mean, old, racist white man who belittled my father at work, and one day my father couldn't take his racist insults anymore, and let him have it. So they packed their things into the car, and all of us left for Nicaragua. My mamá was pregnant at the time. As for the racist white trash, I hope he learned the lesson to not mess with my race. My father left 'cause he knew that a white policeman would arrest him, and a white judge with a white jury and probably one or two blacks would send him to prison. I lived in Nicaragua for eight years before coming back to California. I was a playful kid who often got into fights at school. I must have gotten kicked out of at least three preschools for being a shit-starter.

Unfortunately, my father was not around, 'cause my mamá had left him for his womanizing. My mamá had too much pride, so she packed her things and took my sister and me to her parents' home, 'cause my father was sleeping around all over town. Both of my parents were good-looking, so my father used his looks to get women, while my mamá went on to study at a university. I would hear stories about my father that would make you laugh, 'cause he was quite a character. Later on in life I found out that he was a brujo, unfortunately a wicked one who will be judged by our Creator and by Jesus. As for my mamá, she was a university student, an activist and a teacher, who fought for equal rights for students and working-class people. One day, when I was about five years old, I saw her protesting with blocks full of students, then la Guardia Nacional came to shoot at them and beat them with batons. I saw my mamá trampled to the ground; then she picked herself up and ran up to me to take me to safety. I will never forget that! Later, my mother was blacklisted and was not allowed to teach. So she left to Panama to teach. I was taken care of by my abuelita, tío and tía, who worked with mentally ill patients at a

crazy house. But I idolized my three older cousins, who lived with us. My abuelita and tía taught me to be an individual and have my own mind, and my cousins taught me to fistfight, and encouraged me not to depend on anybody and to never give up. And from my mamá, I learned to stand up for my beliefs, rights and education.

I had a fun childhood in Nicaragua. At a very young age, I liked girls and defended the weak kids against bullies, and I had a violent and stubborn attitude, which got me into a lot of mischief.

At the age of ten, my sister and I came back to San Francisco to live with my aunt, who was married and had two teenage daughters and a seven-year-old son. I started going to Sunnyside Grammar School, but I only lasted a semester due to fighting in school. I was transferred to Glen Park Grammar School, and got kicked out again. Then I was transferred to Diamond Heights Grammar School, and got kicked out again—but why, you ask? 'Cause little black kids would group together in a gang, and beat up non-black kids and rob them. So when I saw a mob of black kids coming up to me, I would look for their leader or the biggest one, and I would fight as an Apache warrior! The public school never saw it as black kids being discriminating and hateful toward non-black kids. So, proud brown warriors like myself would get kicked out and labeled as troublemakers. I really liked Diamond Heights Grammar School, for I lasted there for one year and I had friends there. During my last week, I came to the aid of a friend, called Danilo, who was little, skinny and wore big patches on his pants. Everybody made fun of him. One day, two black kids beat up my friend Danilo and ripped off his pants. When I heard what happened, I got hold of one of the kids in the bathroom and kicked the living shit out of him. The other kid sent me a girl who stated that I should wait from him after school for a one-to-one. Rumors were going around that I was going to get jumped by the majority of the black kids. Danilo told me to tell the principal and I refused, and demanded for him to stay quiet, for I had to be there and fight them all. I had no other choice but to fight! The bell rang. I was ready to meet my combatants, and all my little school buddies begged me to exit through the back way. I told them that I was not a coward. So I went to meet my foes. I stood right in front, where I was able to get a view of where they were coming from. Then, all of a sudden, I saw mobs of them coming from my left, right and front sides (no back sides, 'cause I was against a fence). I clenched my fists real tight, holding onto some rocks, and as they ran toward me, I punched and kicked as many bodies as I could before dropping to the floor. As I tried to get up over and over again, I was brought down by their punches and kicks, but I managed to grab on to some afros and punched some heads as well. My bus driver came to get them off me. As a result, they all ran in different directions and I was bruised up real bad from their royal ass-kicking. Regardless, I fought back. The bus driver wanted to take me to the office and tell them what happened. I refused, for I chose to fight! Then I begged her not to, 'cause if my aunt found out, I wouldn't be able to watch TV and would receive another ass-kicking with her thick, wide belt. I pleaded with her and told her that I was no tattle-tale, I was a warrior. She was a white lady, so I don't know what she was thinking at the time, but she took me to the store and bought me ice cream. When I got home I told my aunt that I fell from a fence and landed on my face. She believed me, and gave me some steak, while screaming her head off.

When I got back to school, I decided to fight a one-on-one with every kid that jumped me that afternoon. They were shocked and a bit scared, and no one wanted to fight me like a warrior, one-to-one, toe-to-toe. So I got pissed off and started a fight amongst a few of them, and they called for more backup. Then we were taken into the principal's office, and I got accused of starting a riot. Then I got kicked out.

Back at my aunt's house, I was spanked with a belt and was not allowed to watch TV for weeks. That night I cried, for I had lasted a whole year at that school, in which I was able to build friendships with some schoolmates. I had friends to play with in that school and now I was lonely again, no friends and no school.

My mamá gathered enough money, and came to San Francisco, and we all stayed with my aunt. I was placed in a Catholic school. I started the fifth grade. The other kids had been there since first grade, so I was an outsider. On my first week, I challenged the toughest kid in school to a fight, 'cause he and his friends were making fun of me on the way I played basketball. The toughest kid in school was somewhat shocked, 'cause no one had ever dared to challenge him. No one liked me, so every once in a while I got into a fight when someone talked their shit. But in that school, I met my best friend, Gordis, who unlike me had never gotten into a fight. All of us ended up going to the same junior high, a Catholic school. At that school we were like the United Nations, for there were Indio-mestizos, Asians, Africans and Europeans. My peers let everyone know that I was a fighter, and within a couple of weeks I was fighting some new kids. Upon graduating from middle school, I went to one of the best high schools in San Francisco, Saint Ignatius College Preparatory, while all of my schoolmates ended up going to different high schools.

My mamá had to work two different jobs to keep both my sisters and me in Catholic school. At SI I met big-mouth Chino, a tall Peruvian and Puerto Riqueño loudmouth, who became a close friend after a couple of fights. We joined and helped organize a Latino club, in which most members were coconuts. But there were four of us coming from the Mission, and one homie from Daly City. When we were together, the white students feared us, but when we were alone, the white kids would say racist, stupid statements that didn't make any sense. Also, they would write me little notes and leave them in my locker, stating that I should go back to the Mission. They would call me names behind my back, and when I turned around no one would say anything. Sometimes, I would catch them slipping, I would slap their silly grins off their faces. Then I would get sent to detention, showing the whites of my knuckles to Mr. Murphy, a funny, hardass old teacher.

I remember all five of us went to try out for the freshman football team, and we were cut by the third day, except for the homie that had a white man's last name and looked white. Ironically, he was our weakest link. During the weekend, Chino and I roamed the Mission house parties and get-togethers in the parks. And, as always, I would get into a fight, and I would also get a girl, for I was a good-looking kid. These were the best years, because us Raza teenagers were not trying to kill each other, we were just having fun going to parties and going cruising. By this time, I was the Last of the Mohicans at St. Ignatius. Chino's parents realized that the

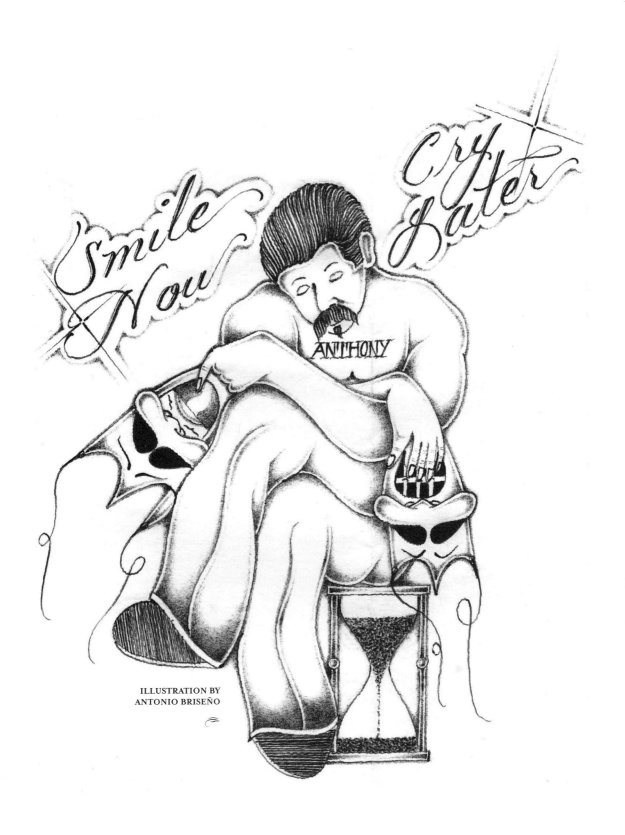

ILLUSTRATION BY
ANTONIO BRISEÑO

Mission was getting too crazy for their little loudmouthed kid, so they moved to Concord. Chino was my best friend at that time, and I didn't keep in touch with the other guys; they had their own little group, and I got myself a girlfriend to kill the loneliness. One day I got into a fight with a prominent white boy at S.I. He started it and I finished it, but at the end I got the boot from S.I. I was deeply sad when Brother Draper told me that I could no longer attend S.I. It was as if he had reached his hands into my soul and ripped it into shreds. I asked if the white guy was going to get kicked out as well, and he responded "You're the problem." I didn't know how to explain my case to him, and how I was proud of who I was as an Indio-mestizo, which made it hard for the white darlings to accept me as an individual. I did not know how to explain to him that every day of the year I heard racist, idiotic comments, and got weekly threatening calls to my house to leave the school, and had my locker where I kept my books sabotaged. I just didn't know how to explain to him that I was a proud Nicaraguenese and that I was a warrior. So I stayed quiet, got up, cleaned my locker and walked away from Saint Ignatius College Prep. I felt like a big failure. I thought about my mamá, and how she had to work two jobs to keep my sister and I in school, and that now I had failed. I waited a day to tell her, and when I did, she was greatly disappointed. I felt depressed, 'cause I wanted to graduate from there. I would have had a white man's education and still would have maintained my identity as a native of "America."

By this time, everybody was clicked up in the Mission District; all the gente seemed to belong to a barrio or a clicka. The majority of young homeboys would judge you on your clicka or the barrio you belonged to. Not me—I judge a vato on his cora, courage. I wanted to belong to something bigger than myself and be accepted by my peers. I didn't get it from school; still I kept on striving, trying to succeed in my schoolwork, inspired by all of my obstacles. I wanted to be greeted as a carnal, so I turned to my local neighborhood for acceptance, but my bullheadedness and my way of defining a "man" kept me from being truly accepted in the barrio. First of all, to put it bluntly, my barrio was weak; only a couple of us had a warrior's cora, while the rest were just talk. And I thought I would change that, so I fought everywhere I went, and little by little my so-called homies were not strolling beside me anymore, 'cause it was suicidal to walk with me. There were times I would run up to 10 or 15 vatos from a rival barrio and throw blows, and no one was with me.

I was known as a vato that would fight anyone, and it caused jealousy with those that had no cora. I was truly respected by some older vatos that crossed my path. I traveled all over Califas, from San Fran to Santa Rosa to Barrio Logan Heights, San Diego. I loved to travel, and whenever I got the chance, I grabbed my bags and off I went, in spite of all the wars. But not everything was fight, fight, fight. There was a whole lot of fun and babydolls as well. I had a good homie by the name of Lucan, who was from my barrio. Lucan was a Casanova, and avoided fights like the plague. When we both went out to get some babydolls, we pulled them in like bees on

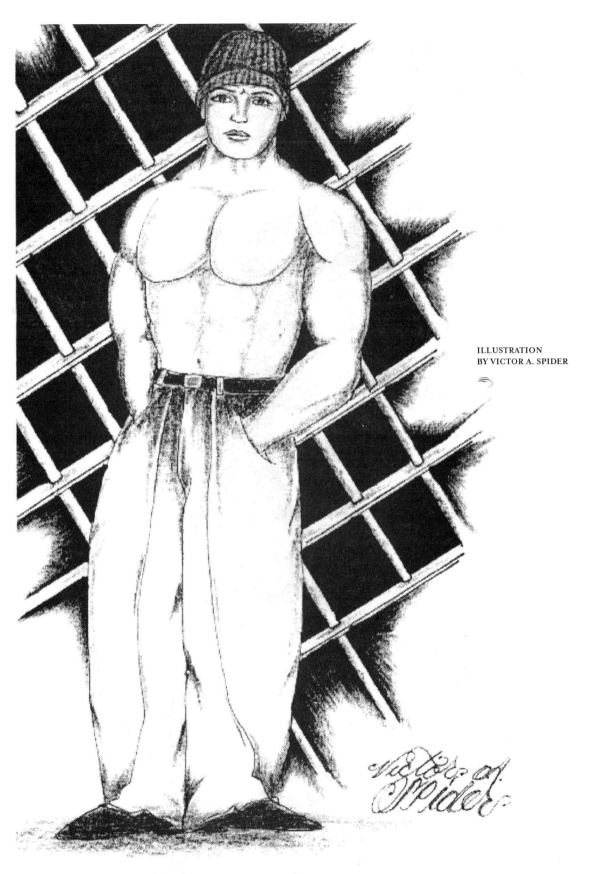

ILLUSTRATION
BY VICTOR A. SPIDER

honey. We were two good-looking vatos, and it was easy for us to get laid, bottom line! One thing about us, both of us would try to win over the finest babydoll from the group. Sometimes I got the finest one, and other times Lucan did. It didn't matter where we were. Malls, schools, streets, parties, clubs, etc.—we reeled them into our arms. I remember on one night on Broadway Street in San Fran, Lucan and I ran into a group of hinas, and we both started talking to the best-looking one. Then I gently grabbed her hand, pulled her aside, and told her "I choose you among all others." Then I kissed her. And before you know it, we were driving to Richmond to get laid. Lucan went to the other girl's house, who also lived in Richmond. The babydoll snuck me in through her bedroom window and a rosebush messed up my firme Pendleton shirt; man oh man was I pissed. But the hina took care of me real firme and I gave her pleasure as well. Next morning, I heard a woman's voice and a hard knock. She panicked and told me to go inside the closet. Then she opened a little cellar door, and I dropped through to the foundation of the house. I saw a couple of mouses running around. Minutes later, she opened the little door and came back to her bed. Later, she waited for everybody to leave, cooked me something quick and drove me home. Plus, she gave me some money so I could get my Pendleton fixed up. I saw her again just one more time, and moved on. Now, homie Lucan had it gacho.

"Hey Rey, I almost got my ass kicked by the hina's jefito. It was fucked up, holmes! He saw me going into her room and started chasing me, telling me he was going to fuck me up. I ran across the street and hid behind some bushes. I stayed there all night 'cause he was guarding the house," exclaimed Lucan. "You punk, why didn't you get up and kick his ass, ha ha ha!" I said. "He was a big-ass motherfucker, fuck that holmes. Then, next day I had to walk to the BART, and some pinche mayate gave me the wrong directions and I got lost. I got all kinds of blisters." I just kept on laughing, picturing Lucan hidden among the bushes from some hina's father, looking to kick his ass. My homie Lucan and I had many fun adventures! Hinas from Santa Rosa all the way to Longo (Long Beach). Que ondas pinche Lucan, shaaa!!

Now let me take you on some not-so-pretty adventures. The barrio I belonged to was Ghost Town, and one night we received word that the ESDC Boys and the E Boys were coming down to the Mission to bust a few heads. So a few of us got together and headed to ELE PE, to meet with ELE PE and throw chingasos with the rivals. We waited and waited; the ELE PE vatos were talking about my barrio being an extension of ELE PE as the pee wees. I liked the idea, 'cause ELE PE were respected and had great pull with babydolls from all over Northern Califas. Then I thought, shit, I could move up quickly by busting a few heads. But my barrio disapproved of the idea. After waiting for quite a while, some vatos left and a few sparked up PCP. Minutes later, a deep caravan of about seven cars and trucks filled the street with ESDC and E Boys. They got off their vehicles with knives, chains, bats and other weapons. I said, "Here they come, let's get ready to battle!" Then my so-called homies shit their pants and ran! I yelled "come back and fight!" So I had to make a stand by myself. Within seconds I was completely surrounded, showing no signs of fear. The main vato from ESDC demanded, "Where you from, vato?" I raised my head and clenched my fist, and said, "I'm Reynaldo de Barrio Ghost Town aquí caigo." Then a big ugly-looking guy from the "E" said "I'll eat you alive!" And the beat of fear that was pumping in my chest boiled my bloodstream into anger and, just when I was about to say something, the main vato from ESDC said, "This little vato is a warrior. You got balls, carnalito. You remain standing tall with the big ESDC and the E. Them vatos that left you are cowards. They are not your homeboys." Then he put his hands on my shoulders and said, "Go back home, little vato, and stay strong." They opened their circle and I walked away with my head down, feeling gacho like a gavacho with my pride hurt. Then, all of the sudden, that same vato said, "Raise your head, proud little vato, and walk proud. You got balls, homie." But I couldn't, because he was right, my barrio was composed of cowards, so the tears of a clown were shed upon my face as I walked what seemed to be a long, lonely road back home. Later, I had my own personal battles with the E Boys. Simon, just little ol' me and their whole entire barrio! I never asked for any backup! It was not in my nature.

As the wars among barrios and clickas grew, Ghost Town decided to stop existing, 'cause frankly speaking, it didn't have the balls to remain strong. The few homies that were warriors left to join other clickas. I organized our last junta to try to gather a few vatos and start fresh. Only two showed up. An hour later, Tomás and Wolf told me, "Go home, caballo, it's all over." They left while I stayed, gazing into the mystical sky, wondering what was to become of me. I had no barrio. Then I looked at the site where I got jumped in tears, and a smile came upon my face. Then I remembered getting stabbed in the back by an ex-girlfriend. I was ashamed, for it didn't happen in battle, so I never told anyone (because of my lifestyle I would get a lot more stab wounds from "syndicate" vatos down to street hoodlums). But later, Lucan found out, and I threatened his neck if he told anyone. I remember vatos that I had fights with coming up to me saying they didn't do it. I remember waking up in horror 'cause I had a big-ass plastic tube in my penis, screaming for the nurse, asking what had happened to my family-productive organ, and the nurse nicely explaining that it was OK and that I would be able to have sex and have kids. Investigators came asking questions, and I asked them to get the guys that did this to me and bring 'em to me, so I could kick all of their asses, 'cause I was too drunk to know who stabbed me. Then I told them to leave me alone! Then I remember my old friend Gordis and his homies paying their respects, looking all sad with their heads down. I told Gordis "Stop looking so dead, you're making me feel all depressed. Shit, Gordis, I'm not dead!" I asked them to turn on the TV and to look for some music to liven up the room. And all we saw were clips of a funeral and some band singing "Another One Bites the Dust." All of a sudden, we started laughing so hard that I needed a shot of painkillers.

ILLUSTRATIONS BY VICTOR A. SPIDER

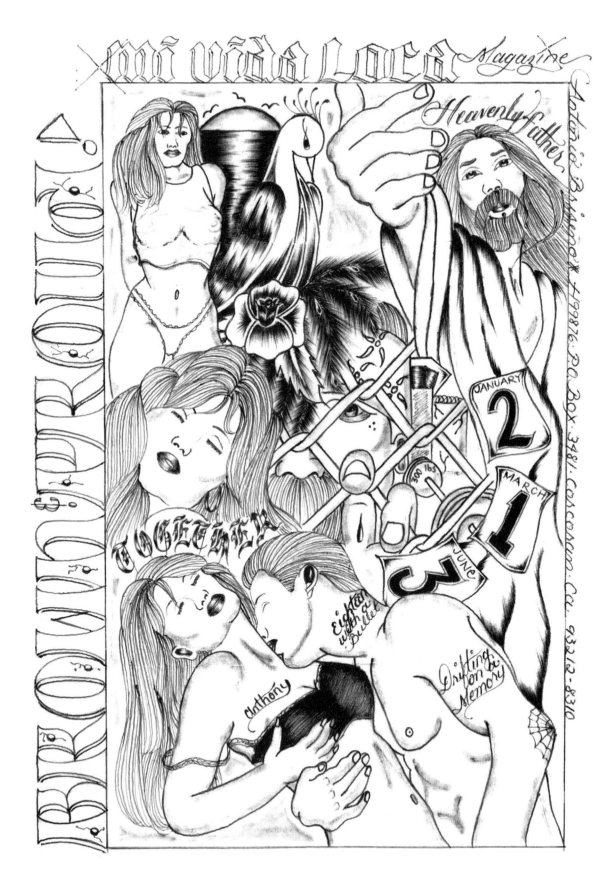

ILLUSTRATION BY ANTONIO BRESEÑO FROM SOUTHLAND (PAGE 16), ILLUSTRATION BY VICTOR A. SPIDER (PAGE 17)

Now my thoughts came back to the present and I felt lonely. No girl, no homeboys and no barrio to belong to. As I kept on gazing into the sky and stars, I told the Creator that I would never join another barrio again. I would remain my own man. I would be my own island. I would fight those that disrespected me and befriend those that extended their hand to me, no matter where they were from. From that day on, I became my own island, and was guided by machismo. I must have been 16 years old at the time. The next day, I told my mom that I wanted to change and that I wanted to go see my father in Salt Lake City, Utah. Within a couple of days, I enrolled in a high school in Salt Lake City. By the third day, a white guy came up to me and said, "Hey vato, do you have a low rider?" I was stunned, and was left with my mouth open. I got myself together and asked him, "How do you know that I'm a vato, and how do you know about low riders?"

"There's a lot of cholos on the West Side, and they all go to school over there."

After school, I ran back to my father's house and told him to transfer me to that high school. He answered, "Are you out of your fucking mind? You're in my house, and I set the rules. No son of mine will dictate to me." Then his woman told him to calm down, which he did, and then said, "I don't want you with the cholos, 'cause you're going to get in trouble. You chose to be here to change your fucked-up ways. Stay at the school I enrolled you in and forget about La Choleria. As a matter of fact, don't wear those big-ass pants anymore. Let's go to the clothing store and I'll buy you some new clothing."

So off we went, and he bought me some tight pants looking gay as hell, with some off-the-wall shirts. The next day, I put on my new clothes. I must have walked half a block and decided to run back to my dad's house out of embarrassment for looking so gayish. So, I put on my creased-up Pendleton shirt and razor-creased, baggy Frisco Ben pants. When I got back, my dad saw me and said, "I'm the only man in this house. Everybody else will have to cut their huevos and hang 'em on the door, 'cause I'm the one in charge. And if you don't like my rules, you can leave!" Immediately, I answered "then I'll leave!"

"Juana, go to the bank and get some money. Buy him his Greyhound ticket back to San Francisco," said my father. I packed my things, and in less than a half hour, I was at the Greyhound station. Before departing, Juana hugged me and said, "Your dad loves you, it's just that he is very strict. If you would have been raised by him today you would be a different person." Then I answered, "I think I would have left long ago, just like he did, when his father enforced the house rules."

When I went back to Califas, I enrolled in Downtown High, a continuation school. I attended school for four hours and went to work the other four hours. One day I went to talk to my school counselor, 'cause I wanted to become a pilot for the Air Force, and he said, "That's for people who go to college; it's better if you enlist in the Air Force and fix the planes." I quickly responded, "I don't want to fix them, I want to fly them and put Geronimo's name on it." And then he re-stated that I was not college material. Right then and there, I decided to get my high school diploma as soon as possible and go on to college. I went on my own to find out how to enroll in college all by myself.

But I still had the shame of getting stabbed by a "broad" and being a barrioless vato. So I saved enough money and bought myself a ticket to the land of Sandino, Nicaragua, named after Nicarao, a fierce warrior who fought the Spaniards. Upon my arrival in Nicaragua, when I exited the airplane's doorway I received a huge slap from the tremendous heat. The country had just beaten the U.S.-backed Contras over their decade-long civil war. Men, women and children were waving the red and black FSLN flag. I didn't comprehend anything about politics back then, but from what I saw people were walking freely and looked happy. I saw a lot of men and women wearing uniforms, and none of them ever bothered me or questioned me. As a matter of fact, people looked at me weird because I had a shaved head and wore creased-up baggy pants. My tía told me that I looked as if I'd run away from the crazy house, and so I was given some straight-leg jeans to wear. I wanted to make some friends, but people looked at me as if I was a monster. I remember being in the bus with my uncle, and this guy just couldn't keep his eyes off me. I tried to avoid him, but the guy had his eyes locked on me, without blinking! Finally, I got up and told him, "If you don't stop looking at me, I'm going to rip your fucking eyes out of your face." Finally the guy stopped staring. My uncle told me to calm down.

One night, I went out drinking with my older cousins, and I really got blasted on Flor de Caña rum. Somehow I managed to get us kicked out from the place where we were drinking. My cousin grabbed me and put me on his shoulders. I began to hit and kick him, telling him to put me down. Soon, he threw me on the ground and left me in a barrio called "Barrio Maldito," where thieves rob other thieves, and where police don't go unless they have a machine gun. I remember going into someone's house, pulling the guy off of his bed and laying on it. Then a lady chased me out with a broomstick while screaming to get the hell out.

The next morning, I woke up inside the cemetery, with my clothes torn and one shoe missing. I remembered the cemetery from when I was a kid, so I knew where I was. A family member lived around it. I asked for Doña's Paula's house and was directed right to it. She received me with open arms and gave me a delicious meal, then she had a nephew escort me to my tío's house. A couple of days later, I was at my older cousin's house and they gave me a big lecture on not handling my liquor, and then they focused on my stabbing from my ex. One of them said, "When you get back to the U.S., kill the bitch and dump her body in the ocean." My second cousin said, "Go and have sex with her as if nothing happened. Then kick her ass so she will never ever think of it again and dump her right there and then, but make sure you fuck her real good and kick her ass as well, OK?" And my third cousin said, "Do not under any circumstances see that bitch again! If you see her on the streets, look at her as if she's shit. One day, you'll see her again, so act as if nothing happened. Just make yourself happy, that alone will kill her." And he was right. Years later,

ILLUSTRATION BY
ZEPEDA FROM GILROY

I saw her all torn up drinking at a bar, while I was using the public phone to meet my fine-ass girlfriend. I didn't even recognize her. She said, "Reynaldo!" I turned around and there she was, looking fat and raggedy. Funny, right away I felt sorry for her." She said, "Damn, Reynaldo, you haven't changed. It's been years and you still look fine. Guess what, I'm married to a Nicaraguenese and I have two kids from him." Then I stopped her and told her that I had to go. Then she asked if she could hug me. I felt sorry for her, so I said OK, as long as she didn't have a filero. She gave me a bear hug and began to cry. Then I said, "Show no emotions, it's stupid." Then she said, "You're still the proud chingon que le vale nada." And as I walked away, she screamed "Your pinche pride will take you to your grave one day!"

Now back to the other story, when I came back from Nicaragua, I felt rejuvenated, motivated and more assured of myself. I resumed school and research about college. I went to house parties, strolled the Mission, and got into some adventures.

One day two homies from Logan Heights, San Diego were in town. I knew them from before, and we had partied. Our primary goal in life was to pick up on the babydolls without giving up honor. Frisco had met some babydolls from Richmond, and they were inviting him to a house party there. We all met at the "Dork's" house and six of us rode in my 1950 Chevy. We were Frisco from Logan Heights, Zorro from Logan Heights, Mando, no barrio, Jose, no barrio, Gordis and myself. I parked my bomba two blocks away from the party, with wheels facing the "get away direction" just in case. We had some weapons in the trunk just in case we got attacked by the whole neighborhood in another city. We walked into the party with double-breasted French coats, highly polished shoes and razor-creased pants. People were dancing, and a few fine mamácitas came running up to us and greeted us. Frisco made the presentations, and the local Richmond boys were pissed off! Right away, Frisco said "I smell pedo." "Don't trip, I'm down!" I replied. Frisco smiled, confirming what he already knew. Mando and Gordis were afraid and kept on saying that they wanted to leave. Naturally, I told them to fuck off and get a hina.

The hinas escorted us to the keg, and after a couple of drinks, I picked out one of the fine ones and began to dance. We were dancing in the middle of the floor. Then I grabbed her by the waist and pulled her toward me to kiss her. We kept on dancing, when I felt someone bumping me, but I didn't trip, 'cause it was a mistake, I thought. Then I felt another bump. Then by the third rola, a vato stepped on my shoes. Right there I knew that those shoves were intentional. So I looked, and it was this big-ass monster-looking vato, so I punched him right in his face. He grabbed me and picked me up, and I hit him with all I had, so he threw me to the floor. I knew he was hurting, 'cause he didn't retaliate. As he stood still for a few seconds, most of the fine hinas got between us and demanded the vato and his homies to leave. They left, and the babydolls got me some ice cubes and started babying me, but I took it as weakness, for I had too much machismo bullshit, and I said, "I'm going out after him." Mando and Gordis and the babydolls pleaded with me to stay. Then the fine babydoll I was dancing with said "Don't go out there, they have guns and are waiting for you guys to come out." The jefita of the house offered us to spend the night, but my false sense of pride didn't take the invitation, and commanded the guys to go out and battle. They had two choices: Stay, or go with me, and I'm the one with the car, so they went out with me. We scanned out the premises carefully for any signs, and saw no sign of them. Then I said, "Fuck them chavalas, they have no heart. Let's go back in and party with the babydolls."

"Chale, it's the wrong movida, 'cause they will go for more backup and cuetes. And we have no cuetes," stated Frisco. "Yeah, they probably spotted your bomba and they want to shoot all the windows," said Mando. So I ran up to my bomba and I was happy to see it as I left it. Everybody said, "Let's get the fuck out of here, we'll have everyone from Richmond out here, fuck that! Yeah, Rey, they have cuetes and we don't even have a B.B. gun. Nos fuimos." Once we were inside the bomba, I turned around and headed to the house party, and Mando, Gordis and Jose were tripping. I said, "I got to have that hina's number, fuck them chavalos." Then, out of some bushes popped out a big-ass monster-looking vato positioning a shotgun toward us. He shot it, and everyone except for Frisco was saying "Flip a bitch and get out of here!" Then Mando grabbed me by the shoulders and said, "Please, let's get out of here, please don't let me die." "I'm running his ass over," I said. So I tried to hit him, but he went back into the bushes and they started shooting. Then Mando said, "Your bomba, they're going to shoot it. Please, Rey, let's leave." Then everybody started screaming, along with Mando. So I flipped the bomba, while they blasted toward us. I had no other choice but to laugh. Then Mando and Gordis and Jose were just plain terrified. Frisco and Zorro were used to it in Diego Town. Once we got out of harm's way, we were lost someplace in Vallejo, and Zorro pulled out a bag of marijuana and said, "I know you don't like this shit, Reynaldo, but I need it." Within minutes, everybody was smoking, including Gordis, a drug-free type of guy. Gordis said, "You need to be on something to hang out with Reynaldo." Then we all started laughing and laughing. The we all made fun of Mando on the way he was screaming when we were getting shot at. Man oh man did we laugh. Before you know it, I started smoking, then it was a moment of silence, and out of nowhere we all just started laughing and laughing. We laughed all the way back to San Fran.

Months passed and summertime began. I decided to go down to Logan Heights, Diego Town, to visit Frisco and Zorro. Mando, Jose and I went there. They came to pick us up from the Greyhound station with a huero from the Navy, who was a great buddy of Zorro. This huero was from a southern state. Zorro showed the huero how to dress, but as we walked through Barrio Logan all eyes were on me! Frisco advised me not to say that I was from San Fran, 'cause it would get ugly, but I strongly disagreed with him. So I was ready for anything. I was pretty pissed off about that, but nobody approached me on that day. They just gave eye-to-eye looks, and I did the same. When we got to the canton, Frisco and Zorro were arguing over the barrios' politics concerning me, and I told them that I didn't give a fuck and if I was going to get hit up, I was going to tell them where I'm from, 'cause I was not a chavala. The following days, I was not shown around the barrio, and that got me pissed. Finally Frisco set up some dates for us with hinas from National City, and we were to meet them at an arcade near San Diego City College, for they were college girls. Zorro and I were playing the arcades while Frisco went to get the hinas. We were waiting for quite a while, we stepped outside to see if they were coming, but instead Zorro spotted three carloads of National City boys. We went inside the arcade looking at each other.

"Are you ready, Reynaldo?" asked Zorro. "Siempre estoy liste," I answered. We stood side by side as the National City boys slowly came in, blocking the doorway. "There's only two ways you chavalas will get out of here. Either you putos get on your knees or you get carried out!" stated the National City boys. Zorro and I grabbed a chair each and started swinging and hitting them. Then Frisco showed up with two of his homies and chased the vatos away. The hinas never showed up, and Frisco said, "We are always getting set up and we need to be careful when we go out on dates, never tell them where we live. Más al rato, I'm going to introduce you to some good homies, but you have to tell them that you're from East Los. Anyways, you look like you're from East Los." The time came, and we drove into a parque during the night. There were a couple of ranflas and a few vatos. Immediately, I was introduced as Reynaldo from East Los, and it bothered me, 'cause I was from San Fran. The two vatos asked, "How is it in East Los, homie?" Quickly I said, "I ain't from no fucking East Los, ese. I'm from San Fran. They gave me a puzzled look, and I stated, "Tu sabes, the Golden Gate Bridge, cable cars y todo ese. San Francisco, Norte Califas, Alcatraz Island. The home of all the culeros, but I'm a man, ese." Then they looked at each other while I stood in a stronghold position ready for chingasos. And one vato asked, "How is it over there, homie? We never leave San Diego. We figure we might get killed out there in another city." Then I told them about the weekend cruising on Mission Street, and that San Franeros were known as Casanovas, and so hinas were coming to the Mission District from all the surrounding cities. They just looked amazed, 'cause all they knew was Barrio Logan, San Diego. Then one vato added, "It's firme, ese, backing up homie Zorro from them putos." Then I said, "Frisco and Zorro are my comaradas and I back up a comarada." Then we all began to drink. Now, if a vato don't have the huevos to say where he's from, then stay home. Everybody from Norte to Sur Califas and El Paso, Tejas knows I'm from San Fran. And many times I was not well received. After a couple of hours, we all caravanned to see what we could get into, and we just ended up drinking with some other Logan homies at some railroad tracks.

One day Frisco said, "I got the hookups with some hinas from Oceanside, we'll pick them up at their houses and take them to a park." That evening I picked the one I liked, but it was hard, 'cause they were all looking firme. She gave me a smile and said, "I liked you from all the other guys." Then I said, "Hey, that's my line, and I chose you from all the rest."

"You're fine," she said. "How many old ladies do you have waiting for you in San Francisco?"

"What I left behind, stays behind. I'm looking for someone new. It could be you," I answered. Then we began to kiss. We got busy on the park bench under the bright moonlight.

On one weekend, we all went to a Quinceañera thrown by Logan Heights, and Frisco was worried and told me not to start any pedo, so I gave him my palabra that I wouldn't. As we arrived, the hall was packed with Barrio Logan homeboys and some fine babydolls. As soon as we got in, Frisco and Zorro greeted all of their homies and introduced us as their primos. Everything was going firme, and all of the sudden I spotted the finest Chicana from the party. She had feathered hair going to her shoulders, big brown eyes with curvy eyebrows, and a fine, spotless, smooth-featured face. She had a small skin-tight blouse and some tight jeans with heels. It was passion at first sight! I told Frisco that I was hitting her up, and Frisco said, "Chale! She's a carnal's prima!" I walked up to her while the DJ was playing a slow jam. I made eye contact and she did as well. We didn't blink. I walked up to her, gently picked up her hands and asked her to dance. While we were dancing, I felt as if we were the only ones on the dance floor. She asked me who I was, and why she hadn't heard of or seen me in L.H. I answered, "Saves que, mija! The great one from up above has brought me here tonight all the way from the San Fran Mission District, so we could meet and never let go of each other." She gave me a sweet smile of approval and I was in paradise.

We must have danced three slow songs, and then the rola "More Bounce to the Ounce" played, and I started our "own" style of dancing to such rolas. Naturally, I caught the eyes of other eses. Then a vato got near us and said, "Where you from, vato?" "San Fran!" I exclaimed. "You're a Norteño!" he shouted. Then I pushed him hard and all kinds of gente got between us. Then the guy said, "You're in my barrio, ese! And you're not welcome here in our party. And I'll fuck you up right now, le va!" Then Frisco managed to get between us and whispered in my ears, "He's a chavala, he's doing this 'cause he's related to a carnal and the whole barrio is here. If you fuck him up right now, I'll never stop hearing from the homeboys that I brought a Norteño to fight a homeboy, at our own party." He paused and said, "Don't fight him, Rey, Zorro and I will be fucked." So I gave the guy a mad-dog look and walked toward the exit. It seemed like a long, long walk, while the guy said, "Chavala!" My pride was hurting. Frisco said, "That punk is a straight chavala, he did that because the whole barrio is there, everybody knows he's all talk. Thanks for not smacking his big mouth!" To add more insult to my pride, the police came, three cars putting their headlights on our eyes, leaving us temporarily blind. They had us against the wall while a few of the cowards had their weapons pointed at us. I told them that I was from San Francisco, but they did not believe me. So they took pictures and put me in the gang files as a Logan Heights gang member. Years later, I found out that it's illegal for cops to take pictures of juveniles, but when it comes to La Raza the cops break all the rules, and break the law, so we can end up in jail. As for the fine babydoll, I never saw her again.

AZTLAN

3.

VIVIDLY, I REMEMBER

A few years later, I went on to a community college while working full-time, and being in the reserves. Then I went to San Francisco State University. By this time, I was running with vatos from all over Califas and Tejas. Eventually, I graduated with a business management degree and created and founded *Mi Vida Loca* magazine.

Vividly, I remember being in one of my business management classes. We had to give a presentation on a U.S. business corporation. One student, in particular, stated that all the illegal aliens were crossing the border to steal American jobs and that something should be done about it, or by the time "we" were to graduate, "we" wouldn't have any jobs left. My first reaction was to jump up, grab his throat and choke him with his own tongue, then grab my chair and bash his head until his brain popped out so I could spit on it! But instead, I took control of my anger and held on to my chair. I waited and waited until the class was over and I was the last one in the room. A few moments later, I went straight to the canton. I took out all of my Chicano and Latino books and started my research. That weekend I stayed home, no partying!

The next time the class met, I raised my hand and said to the instructor, "I want the floor to clarify a comment made about my people." The instructor was surprised 'cause I hardly said a word in class. I stood up and addressed my classmates. "I'm here to clarify the comment that was made about so-called illegal aliens. But before I begin I will give you some historical facts on the native people of this here land and hemisphere called America. In the beginning, my ancestors, the Toltecas, Quiche Maya, Incas and the Aztecs lived in this hemisphere from the North Pole all the way to the South Pole. My ancestors built temples, pyramids and cities. They were astronomers, zoologists, botanists, priests, warriors, farmers and common people with great wisdom and spirituality. They even predicted that foreigners from far away would one day come to our land and invade us, and eventually we would live under their rule. Never without a fight. After the Spanish conquest, we became mestizos—part Spanish and part, though mainly, indigenous. Still we fought the invaders. When President Polk wanted to invade more indigenous land, he sent mercenarios to Central and South America while invading Mexico. My people fought proudly! Central and South America beat the shit out of the gringo invaders but the U.S. put dictators in power to control the másses. Mexico lost the war. They lost because they fought the Russians and French, and had an internal war. Mexico was weak from fighting so much. The U.S. stole more than half of Mexico's land and called it the 'southwestern part of the U.S.' Now the so-called 'illegal aliens' that are crossing the border today are simply coming back to their own ancestral land! They did not venture out on a wooden ship called the Mayflower to practice their religion. My people crossed no vast ocean to get here! We lost the Mexican-American war and became foreigners in our own ancestral land. In addition, 'illegal aliens' have no type of U.S. documentation and most of them can hardly speak English, so they are not going to go to a Fortune 500 corporation and apply for a managerial position! The types of jobs they come back to are in the fields, picking watermelons, lettuce and strawberries so we can all go to Safeway and take them home to eat! They are risking their lives in the fields 'cause the 'land owners' spray pesticides (which are also harmful to consumers) on them. Now, I ask each and every one of you, is this the type of job you are going to apply for once you graduate from college?"

Out of nowhere, tears were coming out of my brown eyes and I said, "Hey, I'm getting emotíonal, so I better sit down."

Everybody clapped. I hope that they remember what I taught them. And when the politicians start bashing "illegal aliens" in the media, my ex-fellow students will remember that we crossed no ocean to get here! We were already here to receive the Europeans. Our right to be recognized as native people of Aztlan has been deprived. The gringo foreigner imported from Europe has kept us ignorant and against each other for too long! Raza, it's time to wake up! Our pride could either destroy us or rise us up to reclaim what belongs to us, Nuestra Tierra! Our birthright, our identity, our past, Aztlan! Cuauhtémoc, a fearless leader, said, "They burned and destroyed our books, cities and language. Please tell our future generatíon the way it used to be, so we can rise up again!" Simon que si, our history will be told in *MVL*. Books and Raza historians will back it up. La verdad de nuestra tierra y gente se va a revelar! We are a proud gente and our uniqueness as men and women goes back to the beginning of time. Let it be known that La Raza did not come from Asia, Africa or Europe. We emerged from Aztlan! Luis Valsez, a Raza writer, wrote:

"Our people are a colonized race and the root of their uniqueness as man lies buried in the dust of conquest. In order to regain our corazon, our soul, we must reach deep into our people, into the most tender memory of their beginning."

A Chicano pinto wrote:

"You have your own way of walking, talking and being which sets you apart from all others because you are not like any other... RAZA, hold your head high with pride that you don't live in someone's shadow."

Aztlan

After the Creator destroyed the three previous worlds, our ancestors came into existence in Aztlan, which is in the southern part of the U.S. The Hopis say that our place of emergence was in the Grand Canyon, west of the Colorado River. After our existence, some of our ancestors established themselves at a place called Pupsovi (seven caves). The Quiche Mayas, Toltecs and Aztecs have a tradition that they came from seven womb caverns. (Source material: *Book of the Hopi* by Frank Waters.)

Upon our existence, Másaw, a guardian spirit, outlined the manner in which our ancestors were to make a migration, which was a purification ceremony. This weeded out the evil brought from the previous world, which the creator destroyed. Másaw explained how our ancestors were to recognize their place to settle permanently and the way they were to live when they got there. All this was symbolically written on four sacred tablets given to them. Másaw said, "Go now and claim the land with my permission." But before Másaw turned his face from our ancestors and became invisible, he explained that every clan must make four directional migrations before they all arrive at their common place, permanent home. That they must go to the ends of the land—west, south, north and east of our continent, to where the land reaches the sea in each direction. And when our ancestors finish their four movements of their migration in our continent, they would come together again, forming the pattern of the Creator's Universal Plan. But he warned them that future generations would be overcome by a strange people, in which they would be forced to adapt their land and lives according to the commands of a new ruler or else they would be treated as criminals and be punished. (The strange people Másaw warned our ancestors about are the gringos who robbed our land and imprisoned our people to forget the "real enemy.") When Másaw disappeared, our ancestors divided into different groups to begin their migrations to the four corners of our land. Raza, don't let anyone tell you we are foreigners, "America" is our land and it has been prophesied that Aztlan and Mesoamerica will be reclaimed by its children. La Raza! Y que!

Our History

Someplace far in the tropical south, no one knows where, lay a mysterious Red City of the South, Palatkwapi. Perhaps it was in Mexico, Centro o Sur America; wherever it was, spirits were sent to give help and guidance to our ancestors. Young men and women were taught crafts and were given religious instructions before they resumed their migrations to the four corners of our continent. The mysterious Red City in the South was a great cul-

ILLUSTRATION BY
VICTOR A. SPIDER

tural and religious center for our ancient ancestors. In the beginning, our ancestors possessed magical powers which they abused and later lost. In time, some tribes forgot the commands of Másaw, a guardian spirit, and settled in tropical climates where life was easy, and developed beautiful cities that were to decay and crumble into ruins. During their migration, tribes left engraved symbols of their tribe's insignia in many different parts of Aztlan and Mesoamerica, our land! During their migration, tribes were divided because certain leaders didn't agree with each other, so they migrated on their own. Most of the tribes did not complete all four of their migrations before settling in their permanent home, so they lost their religious power and standing.

These migrations took place since the beginning of these new worlds, from the emergence of Aztlan, which is in the southern part of the U.S. It has been prophesied that strange people would conquer us and that our people will rise to reclaim our land: "It will all come at the right time by the right people."

Raza, learn our history, for it will aid us in reclaiming our birthright. As long as we let non-Raza and sellouts keep us ignorant and fighting against each other, Aztlan and Mesoamerica will continue being raped by foreign hands!

Educate La Raza. Fight for the betterment of La Raza. Don't sellout! And keep our blood "Brown-n-Proud." We will prevail! El futuro es nuestro. Viva Aztlan! Viva Mesoamerica! Hasta la victoria!

Our History
From *El Popul Vuh, Las Antiguas Historias Del Quiche*
(Translated and modified by Reynaldo Berrios)

This is the history of the ancient Quiche Mayas, that together with other tribes left Aztlan, the southern part of the U.S., into Meso, Central and South America.

As the Quiche Mayas were leaving Aztlan, they said to the Creator: "Oh Creator, look at us and hear us out! Don't leave us. Oh Creator, que estas en el cielo, corazon de la tierra! Give us our destiny, mientras camine el sol y haya claridas! Lead us to the right path and give our people peace, much peace y que sean felices. Give us a good life and existence!" So they traveled into Mesoamerica, to search for their symbol. They heard of the city called Tula and walked toward it. The leaders of the Quiche Maya were happy, for they had found what they were looking for. Asi, pues llegaron todos a la cuidad llamads Tula. Tohil, a Toltec king, received them. Three different tribes united in Tula. When the gente arrived in Tula, they were dressed in animal skin; they were poor, pero su naturaleza era de hombres prodigiosos. In Tula, the Quiche Maya gained great powers and great knowledge. Later, other tribes came to Tula; it had taken them years to get there. It was known that these other tribes had betrayed their ways, and the Quiche Mayas were mad, for after all, our ancestors were of the same familia. So it rained hard,

ILLUSTRATION BY GEORGE SOTO IN PELICAN BAY (LEFT),
ILLUSTRATION BY PINTO FROM SOUTHLAND

ILLUSTRATION BY
VICTOR A. SPIDER

and many of the tribes were extremely cold, but the Quiche Mayas had access to a great fire. There was a big pleito among the Quiche Mayas and another tribe over the fire. Other tribes left Tula; they had all come from Aztlan following their guidance star to the four corners of our bronze continent!

After leaving the great city of Tula, the Quiche Mayas and a few other tribes went to a mountain called Chi-Pixab, where they received their consejos. The Quiches claimed their name by saying, "Yo soy yo, the people of Quiche! And you are Tamub and you are Ilocab, and we shall never disappear, our luck is one." Then they gave names to the other tribes.

While on the Chi-Pixab mountain, they looked at the star that was pointed toward the direction of Aztlan and said, "We came from there but we have divided ourselves." They congregated sadly on the mountain, because they were starving. But they brought with them the spirit of Tohil, Avilix and Hacavitz, their guidance deities. Their deities told them, "Let's go now, we shall no longer remain here, let's go to the forest. It will be a disgrace if our enemies would imtake us." So they left toward the forest. In the forest a pyramid was built to hide the deity. Several tribes—the Rabinaleros, Yaquis, Cakchiqueles, Batenas and many others—gathered together deep in the forest, waiting for their great star called Icoquih. Again, they were sad and cold, recalling how happy they were in Aztlan. So the sun and the stars appeared. The tribes were happy and so they danced and burned incense toward the direction of Aztlan. The priests sang a song called "Camuco."

"What is to become of us? In Tulan we fought each other and separated ourselves, and so we left our brothers. Where are they now?"

Then they remembered Aztlan, where some of the people stayed. They were wondering whether their brothers and sisters had also seen the aurora, which had brought them much happiness.

When you turn on the tube or go to the movies, what kind of people do you see on the screen? Do you see Raza?

When the teachers talk about history and heroes, whose history and heroes do they talk about? Do they talk about our history, our heroes? Chale! Our history goes beyond the pilgrims and their Mayflower. Our people have been in "America" since the beginning of man/woman.

To begin with, we descended from great Inca engineers, Aztec warriors, Mayan astronomers and hundreds of other tribes. Then, we were invaded by the "conquistadores" de España, who were gold-hungry. Our indigenous ancestors took them in as carnales, fed them and gave them a place to stay, but the Españoles were two-faced. They smiled on the outside, while inside they were planning to kill our indigenous way of life so they could steal our gold.

Later, they stabbed our ancestors in the backs by blowing them up with cannons, guns, swords and wild bloodthirsty dogs. They burned and destroyed our cities, temples and institutions. Our way of life, our culture and our world are forgotten memories of the past. Unfortunately, some of our indigenous ancestors helped the conquistadores, for they thought they were cool. Later, the conquistadores used them as slaves. Raza, trust no one who is non-Raza, who want to join our clickas and barrios, for they will betray us.

Additionally, indigenous women were raped by the Españoles and gave birth to a new generation of people called La Raza, a race of half-breeds who were forced to reject our indigenous concept of the world. So as mestizo children, we were insulted, cursed and laughed at along with our Indian mothers. But the mestizos, along with our full-blooded carnales, fought the Españoles and took our land back. Later, the traitors and sellouts who called themselves of "Spanish descent" backstabbed the Raza pride. They follow non-Raza people and kiss their asses. These people are a disgrace to our culture and make La Raza look bad.

Somos Raza, a blend of goldthirsty Españoles and a proud, rich indigenous heritage of Mayan, Inca, Aztec and dozens of other proud indigenous bloodlines. "America," this is not what our ancestors called it. The Europeans called it America so they could laugh at us. As Raza children, we are born into poverty, grow up in violence and die without any hope or guidance. In Aztlan, the southern part of the U.S., the barrio is our country! For our love of and loyalty for it, we died or spent our lives in prison for it. The pendejada has to stop!

If we were really down for our barrios, we would educate our minds so we could buy the buildings in our barrios and help out our gente. No one else is going to do it for us; on the contrary, non-Raza people are kicking back watching us kill each other so they can take over our barrios! For the love and loyalty of our barrios, madres and our pride, young vatos and homegirls unite! Only we can stop the killings that take us six feet under, for no one else gives a fuck. The poverty and violence that we grow up in is to keep us hooked on dope and in the pinta so that non-Raza people can vulture into our barrios and take over.

Remember what happened to our ancestors. Vultures from across the ocean came and destroyed our world and forced us to believe in theirs. Today, as you read this, it is still happening. When you watch TV, it tells you how to look, act, dance, talk and dress. And the sellouts buy into it, but the vatos and homegirls don't fall for their B.S.; we borrow some of their chingaderas and make it into our own style, the barrio style, which tells non-Raza and sellouts that we, La Raza, are a unique people and that our uniqueness must be respected!

In addition, our heroes are not George Washingtons or Malcolm Xs, the heroes of non-Raza people. Our heroes are Joaquin Murieta, Nicarao, Pancho Villa, Che, Sandino, Zapata. Our heroes died for:

The liberation of our land from invaders and back-stabbers.
The respect of our costumbres.
The betterment of La Raza.

So, vatos and homegirls, when we are fighting each other, we are disrespecting our heroes. Respect y pride are things that no one took away from them. Don't disrespect them—unite, for our survival depends on it!

"DRIVE-BY SHOOTERS
WILL BE SENTENCED TO DIE!"

Ora! Now I'm going to touch on a delicate subject that shook up the whole Southland, the subject of drive-by shooters being sentenced to death. I got the palabra on the subject in hand way before it got on the six o'clock news. When the story broke, newspapers were selling like hotcakes. Juntas were set up in parques all over Los Angeles and Marranos were going stir crazy on the scene. "Sureños" and "Maravillosos" told me their thoughts on the hot topic but I chose not to print any of it, because it's all confidential and I honor confidentiality. But here is the message that was not confidential:

A Word to the Wise—
Drive-Bys are Dangerous
to Your Health

DUE TO MANY CHILDREN, ABUELITAS
AND INNOCENT GENTE BEING KILLED
BY "DRIVE-BYS," THE RAZA DOWN
SOUTH HAS DECLARED WAR ON ANYONE
INVOLVED IN SUCH A COWARDLY ACT.
THERE IS NO EXCUSE OR EXPLANATION
GOOD ENOUGH TO SAVE YOU—YOU
ARE AUTOMATICALLY GUILTY AND
SENTENCED TO DIE AT THE HANDS OF
YOUR OWN GENTE.

Monica was ten years old. She went to school during the day and came home to take on the duties of a housewife because her mother was confined to bed due to a crippling illness. Monica had to cook for her two little brothers and mother, clean the house, dress the kids and even do the shopping and laundry. Monica was a remarkable young girl with a lot of heart. Monica is not around anymore. She can't take care of her familia and she will have no future because some scared puto drove by her house and blasted away thinking there was a rival gangbanger inside. Had he checked first, Monica would be alive today. Somewhere out there, a puto walks the streets thinking he's bad. The notch on his gun represents the senseless and shameful murder of ten-year-old Monica—but he'll never admit it. He's a coward.

Raza drive-bys are not our style and certainly not something to be proud of. It's bad enough that we kill each other for no good reason, but when we use cowardly tactics like drive-bys, we risk the lives of innocent people who have nothing to do with our pedo.

The KKK did drive-bys, the Italian mobsters did drive-bys and then the mayates did. But the Chicano still got out of his car, walked up to his rival and called him out to settle the difference like a man. We Chicanos come from a background of warriors, conquistadores, revolucionarios and military heroes. These facts were evident in the '50s, '60s and early '70s, when gangs would meet in an empty lot at a designated time to do battle. These battles were confined to gang members only and there were no guns used in such a confrontation because to use a gun in a hand-to-hand fight meant that you were a coward who couldn't take an ass-kicking. During those days, if you pulled a knife and your rival didn't have one to defend himself, you'd put yours away. That was the machismo way, our way!

If you and ten of your homies caught a single rival in your territory, you wouldn't ratpack him, you would choose one of your ten to give him a head-on, one-on-one fight, because that was the dignified way and made it respectful. Sure, the ten of you could have jumped him and kicked his ass all the way back to his hood, but there is no class or self-respect in ten-on-one.

Years ago, I would see and hear of instances in the pinta where two Chicanos would have a conflict and decide to settle it. The way it was settled was routine. The two men would go into a cell and the best man would survive. Nowadays, the new breed of Chicano, who has lost the old ways, sneaks up behind his victim, slashes him with a razor blade and runs away, or else he gets two more dudes to help hold the guy while he stabs or slashes him.

Where did the Raza pick up these disgraceful habits of combat? Look around you, carnalito, look around, because the answer is "influence." Just because other races prefer to do their fighting from a speeding car, doesn't mean we have to.

CLEAN UP YOUR ACT, ESE! A MAN DOESN'T SHOOT INTO A HOUSE, LATE AT NIGHT, FROM THE SAFETY OF A SPEEDING CAR.

DRIVE-BY SHOOTERS ARE AN ENDANGERED SPECIES!

BEHIND THE SCENES IN "DIEGO TOWN." IN MEMORY OF MY HOMEBOY MARTIN DE LOGAN HEIGHTS

A couple of months passed and I hit the calles of Diego Town. I got off the trolley on a National City stop to meet Nena, my Diego rep. I was supposed to kick it at Nena's canton for the duration of my trip, but she said that her vato just got out on good behavior and she was going to take me to her homegirl's canton. I hit it off pretty firme with her homegirls and got along firme with their homeboys, who dropped in for a few pisto until Nena's vato showed up. We were introduced, and then he said:

"I heard you're from the north, and that you're here to do interviews for a magazine."

"Simon! I'm from San Francisco and my revista is for all of La Raza from north to the south, and I don't give a shit where people are from as long that they are 'Brown-n-Proud,' then it's all firme. I'm goin to Logan Heights on Saturday to interview them."

"You're crazy dog," he said. "Soon as them vatos find out where you from, they are going to rush you. You gonna get fucked up, my barrio been fighting them for years and none of us will go there alone."

Then I replied, "That's a chance I have to take, it goes with the jale but that's how I earn my respect. Later if you get your homeboys together, I'll do an interview on your barrio."

"That's if you make it back, and that San Francisco on your elbow ain't gonna help," he said.

After the turica, we shook hands and he left outside. A few minutes later, Sonia, one of the girls at whose canton I was staying, came in all concerned and said, "Rey, you're in some shit, 'cause Toker just told me that he is going to bring his homeboys and send

LOGAN HEIGHTS:
FRISCO DEL SAN
DIEGO, JOSE,
REYNALDO DE
SAN FRAN,
ARMONDO,
ZORRO DE
LOGAN
HEIGHTS

you back to San Francisco. He thinks you're with Nena."

"What? What a fucking punk. He acted like he was firme and everything was cool and the minute he goes outside he talks máse. Fuck that chacha! Look, I'll stay if you ladies let me stay and leave if you want me to leave, 'cause this is your canton."

"Chale Rey, you're firme and you're doing good for everybody with the magazine and you can stay here as long as you want," answered Sonia.

Then she showed me the room where I was sleeping. That night, I was thinking all kinds of stuff like, Toker will be showing up with his homies to give me an ass-kicking; then I thought he might creep up solo and start blasting me through the bedroom window. So I went to the kitchen and grabbed a couple of cans of food to prepare me for the worst while I was hoping for the best. While I was trying to sleep with one eye open, suddenly I heard a light knock on the door. All kinds of stuff was processing in my brain, so I got a hold of my cans and said, "Quo, quien es?" Then I heard a low, sweet voice. "Rey, it's me, Sonia." I opened the door; she came in and told me that she couldn't sleep. So we kicked it and talked about life in general and then we kicked it real firme.

The next day, Sonia was gracious enough to cook me breakfast and kept on advising me not to go to Chicano Park in Logan Heights. I invited her to go with me but her barrio was at war with the Heights.

Then her firme roommate, Linda, said, "I know your type, Rey, you gonna do whatever the fuck you want regardless. Mijo, I'm gonna do you a paro, I'm gonna page my main squeeze. He's from Oldies C.C. and some of them are gonna be there, so I want him to take you and introduce you around, OK mijo?"

About an hour later, Linda's squeeze, El Cruiser, dropped in. Then he took all three of us on a cruise in his firme bomba. Home-

boy was saying all kinds of jokes. On the way to the pad, I bought a case of pisto and a bottella of tequila. El Cruiser had only a couple of pistos and announced, "Mija, I have to go home to the vieja and kids so I'll see you later. Rey, you be ready tomorrow, I don't want you to be late for your own hanging... ha ha."

After he left, Linda said, "He thinks I'm dumb or something 'cause he tells me he's not boning his wife. But then again, ella ya esta... Just my luck, he had to be married with two chevalitos. Rey, what do you think?"

"Sabes que Linda, when it comes down to relationships I'm bad, 'cause I don't take the time to get to know hinas, I'm just thinking of having fun with them and when it starts to get serious, I'm out. But this I know, he's not lying to you 'cause he tells you he's married."

"Sometimes I feel bad when I see him with his wife and chiquillos on the streets but when I'm with him it's all firme," said Linda.

Then I changed the subject and said, "Que ondas con la nena?"

"Oh that's cold, Rey, 'cause she was supposed to show you around and take care of you but dumb ass Toker is around and she can't escape. De todos modo, we'll take care of you and you can stay as long as you want."

"That's firme, Linda, thanks. No wonder Cruiser is all goo-goo over you," I said.

"And all this time I thought it was because of my big ol' nalgas."

"Well, that too," I replied.

Later that night, we heard loud music coming from a ranfla and Sonia mentioned that it was Travieso. I was introduced to him and offered him some pisto and tequila. He started talking about some of his adventures. He told a funny one when he was blocked off by Logan Boys and to get away he had to drive on people's lawns, "fucking up their adornitos... they were all flying in every direction. A rana's head popping one way, flowers on top of my ranfla while getting shot at without a crease on me."

"Yea, that's why none of the homeboys want to be around you, 'cause you're stupid and you're gonna get killed," exclaimed Linda.

"Don't trip, because we're in the same boat right now," I added.

"Nel homie, you are worse than me, 'cause I got my varrio and a few will back me up and you're hell of far from your homies. When shit get hot, I just go to my tío's rancho and pop up like toast in Diego," said Travieso.

Then we got to talk for an hour about how firme it would be if everybody got along firme, but there's always someone who will "fuck shit up, a cagapalo."

Later we took a cruise to his ex-old lady's canton, which was in his rival's territory. As we drove closer and closer to her pad, Travieso lowered the sounds and we looked for any sign of trouble. We passed by her house and everything looked OK, so he drove to the nearest phone booth to let her know he was close. While he was about to get out of his ranfla, I noticed a vato across the street and told Travieso to stay while I go talk to him. When I got two arms' length from the vato I said, "Qvo, I'm lost and we're trying to find Chicano Park for the happening tomorrow." He gave me the directions from where we stood and asked, "Where you vatos from?"

"I'm from San Fran and my comerada is a Sureño. Are you from Logan?"

"Simon, I'm a Sureño de la Logan," he said.

"Firme, I'll be at the parque tomorrow to interview gente for *Mi Vida Loca* magazine, a straight-up Raza revista. And I don't give a shit where gente are from as long as they are 'Brown-n-Proud,'" I said.

"Hey ese, you're too far away from home," he stated.

"We both know that, ese, and tomorrow everybody else will know, but that's my jale," I exclaimed. "Everybody's contribution matters, 'cause the revista is positive. We keep fucking each other up in the calles as if we don't have brains to think how we are destroying each other, and the gavaches laugh at us and profit from our miseries while calling our race wetbacks. And what do we do? Nada, we just live in our little world and never take the time to educate our minds so we can bring ourselves forward from our own misery."

"Fuck dog, that's deep," homeboy said. "And you have balls! You have to be trucha, 'cause you're a Norteño and you'll get jumped."

"Look holmes, me and you are getting along firme, so I'm sure they'll be more gente like us, who honor machismo and if shit hits the fan, all I ask for is a one-to-one and to be able to leave without getting shot at, that's all. I don't ask for much, homie."

Then he had a smile on his face and said, "If you run into any pedo tomorrow, you tell them that you talked to Flaco, I'm highly respected out here."

We shook hands and I went back to Travieso's ranfla. When I got inside, I noticed that Travieso had a cuete so I told him to put the shit away and go to the nearest alley. Travieso looked puzzled, but he drove to some rail tracks instead, which was even better.

"Check this out homie," I said. "I do a dangerous jale 'cause you just don't know what's going to happen. I deal with gente from all over Califas and shit gets scary sometimes but you know our saying, 'show no fear.' One thing I don't do is carry any cuetes or sacrifice honor, and when pedo arises and there's no other way pues, I have to throw down without any cuetes, solo a los Paros chingasos. Right now I'm doing my jale and guess what? You are going against my beliefs 'cause you might get trigger-happy and shoot someone for something stupid, entiendes?"

Then I noticed a group of vatos coming our dirección about a block away. We were parked at a dead end, so I said, "Look holmes, I see a group of vatos coming this way. You stay here and don't fucking blast. Let me go see what's what, ya llego?" So I walked up to the homies and said, "Qvo, hey you vatos heard the news that the big bad *MVL* magazine is going to be in the parque tomorrow?" It was like I hit them with a right hook, 'cause they were like, "What the fuck?"

"*MVL* magazine, that's me! I'll be here to do entrevista so you fellows look sharp to represent la Logan."

Then one guy said, "Are you really a magazine guy?"

"Simon, *Mi Vida Loca* magazine is run by a loco for locos. Serio pedo homies. I'm out here to check out the place for tomorrow so I won't get lost," I answered.

"None of us ever heard of it," added another homie.

"If you've been in Los Angeles or San Fran, then you heard of it. That's why I'm here, so you vatos could become fans of *MVL*. It's firme, you can send your arte, poems, dedicas," I said.

Then a homie cut in and said, "Hey dog, I do arte and I get down hell of firme."

"Then bring it tomorrow and give it to me and I'll print it

RENE DE ORANGE COUNTY

with the interview. Check this out, I gots to pull descuenta to get ready for tomorrow so ani nos nachamos," I stated. I shook a few hands and left.

When I got to the car, Travieso was amazed 'cause I didn't get jumped. I explained that we as Raza needed to communicate with each other with respect. Then I told him that a few years back, I used to come to Logan Heights 'cause I had two homeboys from here and on one occasion I fought his barrio, to back up my Logan homies. Now it's all different. I had a whole different attitude. Then homie just laughed, saying, "I heard it all." After that we became closer and just talked about loqueras, women and sueños of what we wanted out of life. Later, Travieso got to see his ex, while I waited outside in the ranfla.

Early the following day, I went to Sonia's canton and homegirl was waiting for me. Later in the morning, Mr. Cruiser came to pick me up and said, "Pues que ondas carnalito, hurry up, 'cause you don't want to be late for your own lynching party... ha ha." And he looked at Sonia and said, "She's got a big smile that goes all the way to Tijuas... ha ha." I got ready and off we went. Homie was sure popular, 'cause fine-ass women were telling him to park it and saying hi y todo, so it took us quite a while to get to Chicano Park.

"Look Homie, believe me, I love women, but I got a jale to do so let's head down to Chicano Park and go from there, que no?"

"I'll take you right now, carnalito," he said. "But I'm just going to drop you off, 'cause I got some unfinished business to take care of."

He dropped me off at the tienda in front of the parque. I went inside and bought a Coke, and started drinking it while checking out the scene. I noticed a vato in his state-issued tramados sitting solo, so I approached him and said, "Qvole holmes, I'm Reynaldo de *Mi Vida Loca* magazine and I told a few of your homies that I was coming today." He looked at me with a puzzled look and said, "I ain't from here dog, I'm from Orange County."

"That's Los Angeles, que no? I heard that Diego boys don't like L.A. boys," I commented.

"Just some dogs, cuz..." he answered.

"Yeah, if it's not one thing, it's another," I said. "Seems like our gente will never get along and will always try to fuck shit up. Pero sabes que, don't trip 'cause I'm from San Fran, tu sabes San Francisco. So before you get hit up, I'll be first on the list. I'm here to do some interviews, now si quieres we'll kick it together and watch each other's backs. Anyways holmes, what are you doing so far away from Los?" I asked.

"I just got out, from the joint, and since my carnal moved out here, I came to visit. My carnal es tranquilo, he left the neighborhood to settle down with his familia."

We shook hands and introduced each other. After a few minutes, I said "It's time to go to work, Rene." Then I walked up to a group of Logan homies. Homie Rene was by my side. I said, "Qvo, I'm here to do interviews for *Mi Vida Loca* magazine. I told a few of your camarades that I'll be here today. Is Flaco here yet?"

"Chale," answered one vato.

I told him that I was from San Fran and that the magazine covers todo Califas Aztlan, and that the big question for today is, "What do you think of drive-by shooters being sentenced to death?" Then a vato asked, "Hey dog, why..." The rest of the conversation was strictly confidential so no interviews were permitted, but I was given the OK to interview the hinas that were from other places. After a couple of interviews, homie Rene had to leave. I stuck around for a few more minutes and then I pulled descuenta myself. Upon going to the phone, I realized that I didn't have Sonia's number or address anywhere on me! And to top it off, I had no ride. So I grabbed my head and asked, "What the fuck am I going to do?" Shit, an ass-kicking would be better than being lost out here tonight. So I walked and walked. Let's put it this way, it got dark and I was still walking around all over Diego Town. I walked to Imperial Avenue where a cruise was taking place. I ran into a group of homies that were drinking up and looking for firme hinas. I saw two on a '64 Chevy Impala S.S. and gave them a mean spill, you know, qvo baby... All I got out of it was a ride to the light rail, which I took to the linia, to Tijuana.

AT IMPERIAL AVENUE

I rented a room and rested my feet. Next day, I took the light rail train and got off at the same stop where I met Nena. Then I began to walk, praying to the Creator that I would find Sonia's canton. I prayed like a preacher. Suddenly I heard loud banda music coming from the corner—I looked, and it was Travieso with a babydoll.

"Hey, Travieso, qvo perrin!" I said as I ran up to him.

"Fuck holmes, me asustaste cabron, what you doing out here?"

"I've been walking around like a lost puppy dog since yesterday afternoon. I been praying to the Creator and you pop out. I'm trying to figure out if it's a blessing or una desgracia... ha ha serio pedo, take me to Sonia's."

"Don't trip dog, let me take her to her house and then we'll get something to eat."

While we ate, homie told me that he got into some pedo last night with his homies and that he was going to take off for a while. Later, homie dropped me off at Sonia's, he said his despididas and I told him that one day I would write about this and keep trucha. He left, blasting his stereo and giving a chaaa? I kicked it with Sonia two more days and then I went back to San Pancho.

Interview at Logan Heights, Chicano Park

MVL: What do you do for fun?
Raza: I go surfing at Imperial Beach, go to parties and just kick back.

MVL: You just got out from the pinta, so what do you think of the N/S caca?
Rene: It's not right, we should be firme and united. I'm settling down and leaving all that behind me.

MVL: What do you think of Raza killing Raza?
Ladies: It should not be that way.

Interview at Imperial Ave., San Diego

MVL: So far there hasn't been any pedo, so what's your mission?
Raza: Pick up the firme hinas that are out here.

MVL: There go some firme ladies right there, hasta luego!

POSITIVE AND NEGATIVE FORCES: INTERVIEWS FROM DIFFERENT BARRIOS

I'm a strong believer in our own positive and negative forces—you know, the good and bad balance. We as human beings, with a purpose in life, must control the balance of the good and bad through spirituality (for example, prayers from your corazon). Since we are not perfect (only Dios the Creator is perfect), we will stumble and fall—but as strong men and women, we will bounce back and keep on striving to reach our goals. Yet if we maintain our negative forces higher than our positive forces, we are doomed to self-destruction. Self-destruction comes in many ways, and gangbanging is one way, plus it leads from one negative act to another. The worst thing is that it gets innocent gente hurt, who have nothing to do with the bullshit. And it leaves some of us six feet under, torcido or crippled for life. Even though there's a lot of negativity out there, I try to help water a seed of positivity for homies and homegirls throughout Aztlanville. I just hope we learn something from these interviews and start balancing our positive forces on a higher scale. Now, let me start by giving you gente a little wake-up call with an article called "Varrio Purgatory," by Darren Garcia, a pinto in Pelican Bay, with arte from Victor A. Spider.

Varrio Purgatory
By Darren Garcia

I died yesterday in a shoot-out with a rival gang, so naturally I was surprised when the veil of darkness lifted and I found myself walking down a cement path that snaked through a sea of rich green grass. At first I thought I was only dreaming, but after running a hand across my forehead, I could still feel the gaping hole left by a rival bullet. I knew right then and there that I wasn't dreaming.

Underfoot, I noticed some writing on the walkway. One block read: On September 6, 1996, Jose Gonzales committed the crime of murder against his Raza. As I continued further, three more charges of killing my own Raza and of contributing to the breakdown of solidarity in the Mexican culture.

What seemed like miles of accusations later, I saw two figures in the distance waiting for me. One wore a sombrero; the other was adorned with a richly colored Azteca headdress and robes. I wanted to stop, to turn and run but my legs would not obey. Seconds later I stood before them.

"Buenos dias," the one with the sombrero and funny mustache said. "We have waited a long time for you."

"Who are you? Where am I?" replied Jose Gonzales.

"Don't you know?" the Aztec asked in his Nahuatl native tongue.

"No." I was surprised that I could understand him, for I've never in my living days studied Nahuatl.

"I am Huitzilopochtli, God of War."

"And I am Pancho Villa. From us you have come and by us you shall be judged."

"Why have you slaughtered your own gente?" Huitzilopochtli asked.

"And why have you not honored your familia?" Villa added. "At this very moment, your jefita mourns your senseless death!"

"You do not love your Mexican brothers, the sons of Aztlan!" Huitzilopochtli accused.

"That is not true, I love my Raza!"

"Then why have you sinned against those you proclaim to love?"

"You don't understand, I did it for the varrio! I didn't kill them because they were Mexican, I killed them because they were from another varrio."

My ancestors traded cynical looks with one another. "Did you ever kill any gavachos because they were from Beverly Hills?

"I did not."

"Then why have you done so with your own Raza? Your own flesh and blood?"

"I don't know," I admitted, dropping my head in shame. I could not meet the gaze of their eyes.

"Then you shall burn in Purgatory for eternity!" Huitzilopochtli declared. And with a shake of his fist, the ground below my feet began to rumble violently, cracking the Earth wide open.

"Wait!" cried Jose.

Fire, screams of agony and the reek of burnt flesh spewed forth from the chasm. Unrepentant souls laughed as the gates of hell opened wide for their newest tenant. Above all the agony, above all the screams of terror, I heard a thunderous voice greet me: "Welcome to the varrio!"

Nuestra Young Raza (RV 15 St.) de San Pancho

MVL: How do you young gentlemen view yourself?
15 St.: Future cholos confused. I think of what I want to be and whether I'm going to make it.
J.R.: Future gangster, and right away I think I'm going to jail.

MVL: J.R., that's not firme, you're supposed to stay away from jail. Why do you want to go to jail?
J.R.: So I could stab people.

MVL: Why do you want to stab people?
(J.R. smiles and doesn't answer.)

MVL: Carnalito, jail is not the real world.
J.R.: But San Quentin is.

ILLUSTRATION BY VICTOR A. SPIDER

MVL: Cut the shit J.R.; now tell me something positive when you
see yourself in the mirror.
(J.R. doesn't answer, just smiles.)

MVL: Carnalito, that's what the people in power want us to think,
so we can destroy each other. J.R. you belong in the escuelita so you
can graduate and help your familia and our gente.

MVL: Whenever Raza are portrayed in the movies, we are always
put down so non-Raza can laugh at us. How do you young gentlemen feel about that?
15 St.: It's not fair. If they are going to represent us, represent us as
we are, with pride. It's not right because we are always portrayed as
the bad guys. White people are never the bad guys.

MVL: Non-Raza in power are encouraging us to kill each other.
And they keep on keeping us ignorant on our real history and our
heroes. Now, how could we overcome these?
15 St.: By creating peace, pensar entre nosotros and coming together
and not fighting over a color.

MVL: Is your history being taught in your school?
15 St.: No, they only teach about other cultures, like whites, and
make a big deal for black history and holidays.

MVL: Carnalitos, tell them that you demand to know about our
heroes like Sandino, Zapata, Villa, Che, Murieta, etc. These are
Raza that fought for our tierra y libertad.

MVL: What do you think of Raza people that act as if they are
white or black?

THIS IS YOUR
FUTURE, J.R.,
IN AN OFFICE
CALLING THE
SHOTS FOR THE
BETTERMENT
OF LA RAZA!

VATOS DE LYNWOOD, LOS ANGELES

15 St.: They are sellouts, punks, and they are betraying their own Raza.

MVL: What message do you have for our people?
15 St.: Be down for your culture.

MVL: J.R., what message?
J.R.: Be down for your shit.

MVL: Be down for the betterment of Nuestra Linda Raza, que no J.R.? We are rising up, J.R. Just help out by doing your homework and tell your Raza schoolmates to do the same. Now be down for that J.R.

Oye Raza, saben que, J.R. is only nine years old! There are thousands of young Raza kids thinking like J.R.; that it is OK for Raza to kill each other. Pues the gavacho has succeeded! So go back to the gavacho and tell them that you are doing a good job so that he/she can say that it is our decade while they lock us up. Some of our so-called leaders are letting this type of shit go on because they are either too greedy or don't have enough huevos to rock the boat. And now they are kissing ass to the mayates, while the "Brown-n-Proud" in the barrios are killing each other. Even some Raza college students are helping non-Raza people in their struggle and forgetting about the bullshit that goes down in the hood. Now, when is our suffering and loss ever going to be significant enough? We need you to come to our barrios and empower and educate our future generation. Kissing ass, selling out and diluting our blood will just bury us deeper and deeper!

(*MVL* acknowledges the Raza who are really making a difference, but there are too many backstabbers that are hurting our people.)

Voices of Aztlan in Lynwood, Los Angeles

MVL: This is bullshit, not to be able to kick back at your own canton without getting shot at. What's happening to the peace treaty?
Lynwood: No one is respecting it. It was cool for two months but then it got out of control. They are doing drive-bys, chasing the homeboys with their hinas and kids. Little kids are in danger. It's not the familias fault, but they end up paying for it!
MVL: Two clickas have joined together. How is it working out?
Lynwood: It couldn't be better. There is no difference between us, we are tight.

MVL: Goals for the future?
Lynwood: Get out of here, get my own pad and make money. Kick back when I get older. Raise a family and show the homeboys how to come up the right way.

MVL: What do you think about La Raza getting united for the liberation of Aztlan by gaining economic, political and social power for the "Brown-n-Proud?"

Lynwood: It needs to happen. If our Raza gets together we would control Califas. The barrios would get together, get back the land and have a big loquera.

Lynwood: That's firme. I'm down for that big loquera myself.

Raza: In loving memory of Wicket and Cyclone, RIP.

Gente de Decoto

MVL: What are the conflicts all about?
Decoto: Gente start trouble. They are trying to make a name for themselves. There is no respect.
MVL: The politicians are not respecting our people and yet we allow it. How can we demand our rights?
Decoto: We have no voice in the government; they look at us like shit. Everybody else has their shit together except us. We need to organize!

MVL: Then how can we unite to fight the real enemy (the system)?
Decoto: It's hard when somebody stabs your homeboy, but there's got to be a start. It will take some time.

MVL: How do you vatos feel about drive-bys?
Decoto: I took a bullet on the head, so I don't like it. It's bullshit because you're going out like a chum. It proves that you are scared.

MVL: What are your future goals?
Decoto: We want to start a car club, do something good and have fun with it. Yeah, and prove to the gavachos that we earned it by working hard at it.

HOMIES DE EAST
LOS ANGELES
BOYLE HEIGHTS

MVL: That is firme. Any last comments?

Decoto: Go to school, get your shit done and achieve your goals.

Voices de Aztlan in East Los Angeles

MVL: What are the que paso with drive-bys?

Boyle Heights: Got to do it right, you can't be hitting li'l kids.

MVL: What happened to machismo? When a vato gets off his carrucha, walks up to his rival and handles things a putasos?

Boyle Heights: Fools are strapped 'cause they don't get out of their cars like you say. They are fucking pussies. This is how it is now, before you settled it a putasos, now it's with guns.

MVL: So in other words, our new generation are a bunch of cowards that are afraid of handling their pedo in our traditional honorable manner, face-to-face como los hombres. We are not like any other race that killed kids and women under Western expansion and under Manifest Destiny! We are gente of a great cultura that have our own ways of handling such manners, and drive-bys are not part of our cultura. Our honorable tradition of the Indio warrior tells us that. We are not European Americans or African Americans in which the gavas used cuetes to kill our ancestors and steal our land; while the mayates use cuetes in their warfare. We are unique among all others and our cultura says it all, face-to-face or nothing!

Boyle Heights: Some think that without their cuetes they ain't shit, they say "we're into blasting, not putasos." And what are we supposed to do, stand there and get blasted?

MVL: I know it's messed up, when you are faced with cuetes, and I have no right answer. All I know is that our jefitas, chavalites and viejitos are getting blasted during these acts of cowardry. As, you vatos know, I'm from San Fran and right now I'm deep inside of Sur de Chicanofornia without any cuete! I don't even have a filero. Yet I'm covering a lot of ground out here in East Los Angeles.

Boyle Heights: What does your barrio homeboys think about these?

MVL: Like I said, my name is Reynaldo, the publishing editor of *MVL* and I'm from San Fran. Now, look around, who do you see with me? NOBODY! That says it all! I stand on my own two feet. My purpose for this viaje is to cover the J de Mayo festival and I was told by my carnal that it would be at Lincoln Park. Now, I got to cover all East Los Angeles to find out where it is. If I'm asked where I'm from, I'll say San Fran. I don't have anyone with me and I will not hide behind a cuete. And the only reason I say I'm from San Fran is out of honesty and sincerity.

7.

INTERVIEWS: FROM PINTOS DE CALIFAZTLAN Y TEJAZTLAN

Arturo, a Veterano

MVL: How did you grow up and where?

Arturo: Where I grew up is easy to answer... I grew up in East L.A. until I was 14 years old. How I grew up is typical for most cholos involved in gang warfare. I grew up in the juvenile system till I graduated to Adult Authority at 18 years of age. On my first trip, I paroled when I reached my 29th birthday. I stood out for 11 months again and went back for four more years; paroled again and was back where I now have eight years down. So I guess you can say, I actually grew up in the pinta.

MVL: Do you have a viewpoint on young Raza claiming one thing or another?

Arturo: That's a tough question, Rey, because there are so many things to consider. What sticks out furthest in my mind are gang-bangers doing drive-bys and claiming to be about something. The second thing is our carnalitos and carnalitas claiming Bloods and Crips and walking, talking and dressing like the blacks.

MVL: Arturo, care to explain about the drive-bys?

Arturo: Damn straight. When I grew up, we handled our business face-to-face and hand-to-hand. There was no mistaking your enemy or rival because you got out of your car, walked up to the vatos and told them to their face to "get 'em up." Drive-by shooters are cowards who bring disgrace to their varrio and their people. Raza never fought from long range. That wasn't our style and we had more class and pride than to settle things from a speeding car. We are a proud people. We do things traditionally, like the warriors we came from. It is my opinion that the chavalones of today have lost their self-respect because they mix with other races and have adopted their ways. I am not alone in my opinion. As we talk right now, anyone driving up to the county jail in East L.A. with a drive-by shooting beef is in big trouble with the Raza, and more awaits in the pintas. There is no respect for anyone who back-shoots and especially if his or her bullet happens to take the life of an innocent baby or somebody's jefita. When Raza in the pinta have a conflict with a certain gang, they deal only with the gang members involved directly. When the blacks have conflicts with a handful of white gangbangers, they pick any stray gavacho and then call it a victory. Often the whites do the same. Raza did not bring drive-bys into the game, the mayates did. And our chicanitos and chicanitas think that's the way things are done. If you want to follow someone, mi Raza, follow in the footsteps of your own ancestral warriors, who maintained their dignity and self-respect during wartime and who did not attack from the bushes. That is not our style!

MVL: Now, how about Raza claiming or joining the Crips and Bloods?
Arturo: What can I say to my people that their own skin and heart can't say a lot better? Crips and Bloods are black gangs and Raza has no business in them. For one thing, the blacks teach Raza nothing about warfare. We've been at it a lot longer and we do it better. Another thing is that it is a disgrace to fight against your own people arm-in-arm with another race. To war against your own people is to be a traitor. If you represent Bloods or Crips, it's turning against your own kind.

In LA you don't see Raza in black gangs, and if you come to the pinta "Cripping" you'll soon be "dripping" blood—YOUR OWN! To join black gangs is to give up being Chicano or Chicana and soon you'll notice you are talking like them because you think that's cool. There's nothing cool about a Chicano or Chicana

ILLUSTRATION
OF ARTURO BY
VICTOR A. SPIDER

talking black, for he has lost his identity.

I don't understand why a Chicano or Chicana would give up their estilo for that of the mayate. All you have to do is stop and think about it for one minute. How would you feel about a black who acted Chicano? Is he ashamed of his own race? Does he think ours is better than his? And how could you trust or respect anyone who turns their back on their people, their very own race? Now, what do you think the mayate thinks of you who tries to be like him? Are you his equal? Can you sleep with his women? Or is he just using you for your women?

MVL: Sounds like you are prejudiced, Arturo. Are you?

Arturo: Damn right, but only to the point where Raza begins to adopt their ways and against the threat of Raza losing their identity. Look at the riot in LA over Rodney King. You saw mayates attacking several Latinos! That tells you where their heart is (where we are concerned). To them, deep down inside, we can never be equals, and you youngsters best wake up to the reality that you are useful to the mayate—but when the chips are down, they will sell you out first because you are not really one of them.

MVL: That's a pretty strong statement.

Arturo: Well, I been forced to live with them since I was 14 years old and I've met and known thousands of them, so I guess that qualifies me as an authority. And there's more.

MVL: More? Explain!

Arturo: Take their rap music for instance, the music your sisters, homegirls and primás listen to, that talks about their sexuality! What you're listening to is mayates working on the minds

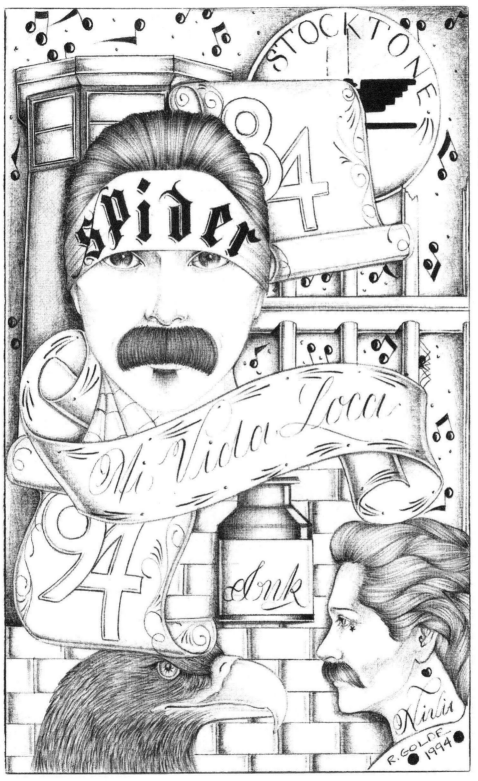

and emotions of your women so that it will be easier to get into their pants. They talk about licking her up and down, entering her from the rear and being able to sex her up all night long. They insinuate through select wording, designed to draw a picture in the minds of our women, that they are sexually superior. If you listen to anything long enough, you'll identify with it and eventually believe it! Who do you think they are directing their music to? Who are they trying to convince? Anyone that will listen to them. That particular type of rap has no class, and you have no self-respect if you allow your carnalas or rucas to listen to mayates bragging about their manhood. You only have to check Raza rappers and compare them to see if Raza shakes their privates at our rucas over the air. You won't find it, because there's more respect there.

MLV: How does Raza get along in the pintas? Why haven't they in the past?
Arturo: There are a lot of reasons and there's bad reasons too; jealousy, control, power trips and greed. You have to understand that the pinta is a different world and the rules are different for many reasons. Personalities clash inside the walls just like everywhere else outside, but in the pinta the conflict can last for years and spread. It can affect the person simply because he lives in North or South Califas.

Raza used to get along years ago. Conflicts arising would be settled and left alone if it was dealt with in traditional Chicano style—man-to-man, face-to-face. In the past few years, youngsters coming in brought a new mentality to settling conflicts: anything goes and everyone is involved. It's called the North and South War. There are too many reasons why the war is on and

CARLOS DE EL PAO (CHUSE), TEJASAZATLAN

one can't put a finger on any one reason. It's safe to say that the war is on for every reason you can think of.

MVL: What advice could you give to the youngsters just coming up?

Arturo: My advice is to forget about pinta life because this world is not the real world, and so it doesn't count for nada. The years I spent looking up to pintos were entirely misguided. You see, li'l brothers, only those who get caught come to the pinta! Think about it, only those who get caught come to prison. The smart ones stay on the calles where the real world is. The smart ones get to see a relationship with a fine brown carnala grow and develop into love. Then they get to see their babies learn to walk and see them grow up. The smart ones get to enjoy life and be part of all the millions of people who do not give up and fail at life because it gets too tough. They also get to make their dreams come true because they were man enough or woman enough to hang with the strong people.

Coming to prison means you couldn't hold down a funky jale or finish school. It means you wanted something for nothing and failed at getting it. It means your world stops and hell begins—in the pinta.

MVL: Anything else, Arturo?

Arturo: Yeah, Rey, writing letters is the only way I can do my part to help educate La Raza. I have a lot to offer and hope to someday find a special someone to help fill this void in my life. So if there are any Chicanas out there who might like to set up on some of this, pues contact Reynaldo and he'll send me your address. Gracias!

Carlos de El Paso (chuco), Tejaztlan

MVL: What's your name and where you from, ese?
Carlos: Yo soy Carlos del East Side Chuco, Tejaztlan from a barrio we called Soco Loco.

MVL: Two years ago I was in Chuco.
Carlos: A lot of gente from Califas come to Chuco because of their relatives or loved ones.

MVL: How have you changed your evil ways?
Carlos: I'm an ex-prison gangmember but I still have my due respects because I gave up all my klicas fuerza y poder for the ways, beliefs and sacrifices of ancient Aztlan. My faith keeps growing and growing. It has no end, only a beginning—sin fin, bro.

I decided I wanted to teach others to see the mistakes we as vatos locos take and end up in the wrong place like prison, the graveyard, mental hospitals or as fugitives. We hurt others and we hurt ourselves. Also, we don't realize the self-destruction till it's late. This is why I want to help others realize that there is a much better way to live: in the name of Aztlan.

MVL: What advice do you have for an Aztlaneco pinto?
Carlos: In the Texas prison system, the reality and concept of Aztlan are misused by Latino prison klicas. The staff watch every move you make. It's very hard to be an Aztlaneco in la pinta because the system fears us. Latino united or divided, we are their threat. Aztlan is alive and is at the moment getting ready to give birth to the sixth sun of Aztec gold. I'm Aztlan.

Spider

MVL: What can you tell us about yourself?
Spider: My name is Spider and I'm from Stockton. I'm 28 years old and I have been rorcido for the last ten. I grew up like most Raza, down with the barrio, los homies and a whole lot of mischief. Like most pintos I was blind to everything but my own needs and, as you see, I've been given a life sentence to think things over.

MVL: In recent years, the younger Raza has chosen the drive-by as the premier tactic of war. What's your opinion of this act of cowardice?
Spider: It's sad. If a vato pulls the trigger on a gun, knowing the bullet may hit a child, woman or any other innocent bystander, how can he justify it as an accident?

MVL: Some Raza have started talking like gavachos and tintos. Some even act like them. What becomes of these degenerates in the pinta?
Spider: Gente asina are called coconuts and they're considered outcasts. If they're lucky a convict will pull them aside and teach them our ways pero most times they end up getting used by those known to us as "inmates." A true pinto will take the time to school these gente right because they realize that some gente grow up blind to our culture. But there has got to be a desire to learn. Otherwise they're left to be victimized by those they've chosen to imitate.

MVL: Why is the Raza separated in the pinta?
Spider: I'm not certain an answer can be given to that question. Not a correct one. I can say it would be a defamation to trivialize it to colors.

MVL: I believe in us, La Raza, and that through education, we will rise to better ourselves, our barrios and our lives. What is your opinion on education?
Spider: Education is the key! In the Ranchera El Rey, it is said, "It's not who gets there first that's important, it's knowing how to get there." I believe education is the way.

MVL: Any last comments for the "Brown-n-Proud"?
Spider: Stand strong, believe in yourself and always push ahead. I'd also like to send a special qvo to the Mexicanita who wrote in to *MVL* and declared her identity. Get on Monica Gonzales, at 11 years old you're showing wisdom well beyond your years.

A FOCUS ON THE HOMEGIRLS

South City Ladies

MVL: What do you ladies want from your boyfriends?
South City Ladies: If we are going to be true and faithful to them, we want the same from them.
 – We want to be treated with respect and for them to be themselves.

MVL: How can you avoid pregnancy?
South City Ladies: By not doing it... using pills, condoms, etc.

MVL: Why do girls give it up so easy?
South City Ladies: This question sounds fucked up.
 – Yeah, but it's true.
 – We are speaking for others, not just because nowadays, a lot of girls are giving it up hell of fast. We are not saying all girls are like that, but most of them are.

MVL: Why have most of you ladies kept your virginity?
South City Ladies: Because we are not going to be like all other girls and give it up to just anybody. When I find the right man, I'll give it up.

San Mateo Ladies

MVL: Why do you think the rucas are dropping out of school?
San Mateo Ladies: They just want to have some fun out there.
 – They don't think about their future.
 – Enemies at school.
 – Some don't think it's that important.

MVL: What would make school better?
South City Ladies: More Latino activities.

– History of Latinos.

– Make it more fun.

– Latinos should start getting along.

MVL: Now, what is this about rucas running away from the canton?

South City Ladies: Taking a vacatíon without permission.

– Sooner or later you have to face the consequences, and the later it gets the worse it gets.

MVL: How do you think a jefita would feel?

South City Ladies: It would hurt them.

– A piece of their life goes with them.

– Your jefita comes first before anything else porque no más hay una madre.

Morena: To all the jainas, remember that your jefita comes first, 'cause your jefita is there forever. Sometimes when a vato is not there or your homies, pero la jefita ayi esta por vida. She's the one that gives you life and us as Latinas, we have to remember that someday we are gonna have morritos of our own. "Payback is a bitch!"

Ladies de Aztlan, South Hayward

MVL: What do you think of the Raza that acts and thinks like the terones and gavas?

South Hayward Ladies: I don't like it because you are supposed to stick with your Raza and not try to be like any other race.

MVL: How can we bring back those of us that are imitating the terones and gavas?

South Hayward Ladies: We don't want them back, 'cause they are sellouts.

MVL: Yeah, but somehow they must learn that they come from a proud race and must stop disrespecting our ways.
South Hayward Ladies: But they do us wrong by backstabbing and disrespecting.

MVL: All right then, start with your homegirl (you know who I'm talking about 'cause she is slipping). Would you ever have a kid with someone outside of our Linda Raza?
South Hayward Ladies: No! I wouldn't understand why. You must stick with your own!

MVL: Now let's change the subject. How many of you are still in clecha?
Christina: I graduated and I'm going to secretarial school.
Crystal: I'm trying to get back into school.
Nicole and Violeta: We are trying to get back to regular high school.
Angelica: I just had a baby girl and I'm still in school.
Jennifer and Angel: We are in regular high school.

MVL: Keep up with your education and never betray our Linda Raza. Any advice for the "Brown-n-Proud" out there?
South Hayward Ladies: Be "Brown-n-Proud" and don't sellout.

Ladies de Aztlan, Santa Cruz

MVL: How do you see yourself a couple of years from now?
Santa Cruz Ladies: I see myself still in but I have kids and it's hard. I'll stay low-profile, but my pride and the high of my Raza

gang is still there just as long as it don't reach home. I'll always protect my family. The anger is there but stupid actíon could mess up my life completely.

MVL: You must always keep in mind that a "stupid actíon" will not only affect you but it will hurt your familia and it will bring them a lot of suffering. As for orgullo, all of us Raza should start thinking of "Brown Pride," which is what our heroes and heroines fought for. They fought so our gente could keep the land and get rid of the Europeans. Our gente fought so we could have a better life with each other; ellos y ellas no fueron a guerra contra los Europeos para que ahora nos estemos matandos como animales. We are a proud people but we need to be proud together.

MVL: Como podemos parar la violencia contra nuestra misma sangre?
Santa Cruz Ladies: Con communicacion!

MVL: Pues simon! Hablando se entiende la gente. Uds. ya saben del pedo que tube con su barrio ase unos meses anteriores y ahora estamos aquí hablando de nuestra linda Raza. Hogala que esta sita sirva para que podamos pensar de nuestra situacion y pensar de nuestro future para que podamos salir adelante. El futuro es nuestro si nos educamos para poder sigir adelante. Pero eso si que cuando venga el tiempo de bronca, tenemos que peliar como hombrio, mano a mano como nuestro antes pasados. Con educacion, unidad y machismo podemos sacar los gavachos de nuestra tierra. Viva Villa, Zapata y Sandino!

Ladies de Aztlan, East Palo Alto y San Mateo

MVL: How is it being a young mother?
Smiley: It's weird because you can't believe it and it puts your life on hold for about 18 years.

MVL: What kinds of things have been on hold?
Smiley: Going out partying, going out with other guys, you know, having a good time like coming home drunk.

MVL: A lot of young hinas think that having a baby, "it's so cute y todo eso," what do you have to say?
Smiley: It's a fantasy. It's not fun changing dirty diapers, waking up in the middle of the night. And you can't do anything by yourself 'cause your baby comes first.

MVL: What do you miss most?
Smiley: Partying every day!!!

MVL: How do you feel being a young mom?
Cynthia: I get up at seven a.m. to feed the baby. I be stressing 'cause I can't do nothing. No clubbing and no partying.

MVL: To all you young hinas out there, que andan de caliente. A few minutes of pleasure will give you years of heartaches and worries 'cause you don't have a job to take care of yourself let alone another kid. Plus you don't have the education or skills to get a good paying job. So think about this and if you think you are a big girl, then be responsible enough to use protection. And remember this always, most vatos are not going to be around 'cause it will tie them down!

(LEFT)
LADIES DE AZTLAN
AT THE MALL
(RIGHT)
LADIES DE AZTLAN,
REDWOOD CITY

MVL: What are your educational goals?
Shygirl: Go to college and become a social worker because I want to help people.
Milisa: I like animals so I hope to travel and work with wild animals.

MVL: How could our gente get along?
Joker: They need to forget about the colors and think about their Raza.
Morena: Everybody has to realize that we are Latinos and that we bleed the same.
Angel: The only way Raza will get along, seriously, is if we put the 14 & 13 aside, but it is not happening. We need to put the signs down and put La Raza first.

MVL: Now, Olga, why don't you go to school?
Olga: I don't like to wake up in the morning.

MVL: Do your parents wake up in the morning to go to work?
Olga: Yeah.

MVL: Then what do you think will happen if they don't get up to go to work anymore?
Olga: (speechless)
Joker: (Olga's carnala) We'll go broke and have no furniture.

MVL: Olga, just like your madre y padre get up early in the morning to bring you up in this crazy world, the least you could do for yourself is go to school so that one day you can pay your own bills and manage your own money.

Angel: For everybody who don't go to school, get your education 'cause I got a taste of it out there and it's hard paying bills, getting fired and not having any skills. It's hard and that's why I'm back in school. I'm taking a nursing program.

Ladies de Aztlan, Jefferson High, Daly City

MVL: How many of you ladies are planning to attend college?
LL: We are all going to college. My mother is saving some money in the bank for my college education.

MVL: Is your school teaching you ladies about Raza history?
LL: No. All they do is teach us about white people. This was our land and they don't teach anything about Latinos.

MVL: There are Raza out there acting like the whites and blacks, what do you ladies think about that?
LL: It's stupid, why be something you are not?

MVL: Your future professions?
LL: Architect, so I could build affordable homes. Advertising. Interior decorator. Pediatrician so I could take care of kids. Counselor for our gangs.

MVL: What do you think of Raza shooting at each other?
LL: It's stupid; we shouldn't kill our own kind. It's just dividing us more.

MVL: What are your messages for the locas and locos?
LL: Stop fucking around. We're fighting over stupid shit. Stop the violence!

Ladies de Aztlan at the Mall

MVL: How do you ladies get treated at Tranforan Shopping Mall?
Ladies: They always kick out all the Latinos that are dressed like cholas. They never kick out the mayates, gavachos, Filipinos or Samoans. They don't let us kick back or let us be in a group. We buy things and they still kick us out.

MVL: Why does the Tranforan security do this to the Raza?
Ladies: They don't give us a reason, they just do it.

MVL: Ladies, organize amongst yourselves. Get a lawyer and bust a lawsuit on them. I'm serio, bust that grape! Let them know the "Brown-n-Proud" are not going to take their shit.
Ladies: Also in school, teachers be favoring other races and when it comes down to La Raza, they make us feel stupid, as if we are nothing. They don't have any Latinas or Latinos teaching, it's racist. Whenever they see a Latino student con tattoo and dressed as a cholo or chola, they think we are fucked up in the head con all this gang stuff.
MVL: Pues what can I say except that we need to come up. In order for us to come up, we need to stay in school and go on to college. Our Linda Raza needs Raza teachers and administrators in the schools. But they must never forget who we are and concentrate on our gente. If we don't take care of our Linda Raza, no one else will. So education is the key and loyalty toward La Raza is first priority!

Ladies de Aztlan, Redwood

MVL: How do you ladies feel that La Raza is being ignored on TV and movies?
Redwood City Ladies: All you see are whites and blacks coming up. There should be an organization that will do something about this instead of talking about it. What you guys do is good.

   – It's disturbing to see that there's a lot of Raza locked up and killing each other (our own people), instead of helping each other to reach the top.

   – If we could have Latino restaurants, then why can't we have more stuff to contribute like more lawyers, doctoras, presidentas, judges and owning our own companies!

MVL: How do you see yourself helping out our gente?
Redwood City Ladies: By becoming a parole officer so I could give our gente in prison a chance.

   – I'll start by being a teacher apollando and educating the youngsters so they can reach as high as they can and move our gente forward and not to kill one another.

MVL: How could we have Raza unity?
Redwood City Ladies: We need to work hard to get there.

   – We need to get more gente like these to talk about it instead of just wishing for it.

   – In order for us to start doing something, we need to respect each other and get along.

   – We need to put aside the norte y sur, red y blue and start acting like Raza.

   – The color we should be claiming is brown.

MVL: Any mensaje?
Raza: Ya es hora de juntarnos!

POSITIVITY

I'm a true believer in higher education. Now that I'm finished writing this here libro, I'm going back to college to upgrade my skills. I already possess a B.A. in business management but this is not enough education in the rat race and so I'll be attending college to become more marketable.

Through *Mi Vida Loca* magazine, I instilled education to the homeboys and homegirls by not only educating them on the past history, but by educating them on present issues. I also organized college tours to San Francisco State University. My friend and counselor, Alberto Oliveras, who was the director of the career center at SFSU, was the top of the *MVL* list as an inspirational speaker who helped me to plant a seed in our gente to pursue college education. Besides the college tour, I was called to do workshops at junior high schools and high schools concerning education, gang violence and Raza history. I networked with community agencies and assisted them to do workshops at juvenile hall to bring some positive thoughts to young Raza who were in custody. Also I attended summits and Raza college days to interview on the que pasos of current political, social and educational issues. Job seminars and employment training were great resources that were also a focus for *Mi Vida Loca* magazine.

Keeping La Cultura alive through the arts, ballet, florico and Danza Aztecas were also featured; as were chavalitos in Raza clubs, sport teams and community organizations helping and educating our people.

The low rider clubs and low rider bicycle clubs is the carnalismo homies share, they are extremely positive in the barrios and they are in a class all by themselves! So I will concentrate on them with their own chapter... Pues aquí les doy, the positivity that's out there in Aztlanville.

College Tour—Ladies From Mission High (pictured above)

MVL: What did you like about the tour?
Gata: I learned more in these tours than I do in school, for example, how La Raza are being discriminated against and ignored by other races.

MVL: What is your comment about the speaker?
Smurfet: I like the way he expressed himself about La Raza. He cares about our people and gives good advice.

MVL: Has this motivated you to think about your future?
Tremenda: Yes, it has, because now I know more about the Raza and it will encourage me to learn more during the years.

MVL Tour—Homies de San Mateo

MVL: What did you vatos learn about the tour?
San Mateo Homies: It is not hard to get into college, you don't have to be an A student.
  – We need to seek opportunities and seek information to come up in this world.
  – The land we are on is ours; we need to be someone big to let the gavachos know that we are going to take it back.

MVL: What did you vatos like about the speakers?
San Mateo Homies: They were kicking down the facts and reality.
  – They were encouraging us to seek out an education. We need more Raza people like that so we can stay in school so we can help out the Latinos.
  – No ay que ser tan pendejos. It's important for us to learn about

Raza things. We need to open our eyes and need to prove the gava-chos wrong, for all they do is put us down.

MVL: Message for our gente?
San Mateo Homies: It is time to stop killing Latinos with cueta-sos and start killing gavachos with knowledge.

MVL: Knowledge! La Raza needs much knowledge and common sense to improve our lives and to keep the gavachos off our path. Knowledge to bring up La Raza and destroy the borders that the savanas have placed in our land.

Mi Vida Loca magazine set up a junta at Kennedy Middle School in Redwood City on education, pinta life and barrio life for La Raza. The speakers were Alberto Oliveras, a career coun-selor from San Francisco State University, Tomás Zuniga, a vet-erano from Watson, Daniel Cuardado, a veterano from San Fran-cisco Mission and Reynaldo Berrios, editor of *Mi Vida Loca*.

Maria: I learned that we must stick together, not to claim and be as one.
Alicia: We should go to school instead of being in the streets all the time. We must be something when we grow up so we can make a better life for our kids.
Jose P.: Those that claim should play games together so they can get to know each other.
Norma: If we united, we would become stronger and our future would be better.
Leonardo: Los problemás que se afrentan en pandillas son con la chota muerte. Tenemos de seguir estudiando, para ir adelante. Echarle ganas y ir a college. Tenemos que educarnos.

Kennedy Middle School, Redwood City

Ana and Selene: No debemos de estar en pandillas porque estamos matando nuestra propia gente. We need to go to school to show people that La Raza can be successful and we need to teach Raza kids about our culture and raise them right.

Campo Kirkpatrick/Miller in Los Angeles County

Homies in the music business like MC Blvd, Mr. Azteca, Sinful, Moses, and the homies from Eastside Productions Mobile DJ Service, along with Create Now and friends, got together for a talent show for the chavalones who are torcido at Campo Kirkpatrick and Campo Miller in Los Angeles County. The homies volunteer to make this event a success. The chavalones participated in the talent show and got down with some firme poetry, art and rap. Each one got their prize including some *Mi Vida Loca* magazines.

It was a firme talent show which shows that every young person has a talent and should be motivated to perfect it and go on in life so we could have a better society. A big qvo to all the contestants...

Voices de Aztlan in Hillcrest Juvenile Hall

Barrios Unidos de San Mateo invited *MVL* to come and participate with the Raza they work with at Hillcrest Juvenile Hall. We were not allowed to take any photos, so Kiki drew this arte of himself and the homeboys who were interviewed.

MVL: What do you gentlemen think about the jale Barrios Unidos de San Mateo?

Guerrero: I like it because they talk about our culture. I have studied the Aztec Calendar and when I get out, I'm going to teach it to the younger bucks. I'm tired of Raza killing each other.

MVL: What do you think about education?

Kiki: In school, they teach us about Columbus and never about what we have done! They put us down in school, saying we are bad. Now, Barrios Unidos de San Mateo teach us about the importance of our cultura, and it is not important what the whites say.

MVL: Tienen que gravarse esto en la cabeza, que los gavas quieren que estemos sin educación y que nos estemos matando para que ninca reclaremos nuestra tierra. When you are in your cell, what do you miss the most?

Yogi: All the girls. I miss talking to them and being with them. And I miss my family.

Guerrero: I miss being free. I miss being with my family. When I first got locked up, I thought I was on the inside looking out. However, after several months of incarceration, I realized that I'm really outside looking in. Being incarcerated is living life outside the real world and society. Every day my family and friends experience life's sadness, joys and sorrows while my life seems frozen in pain.

MVL: What would you do different to keep yourself away from here?

Smurf: I don't know because I've been around the barrio all my life. I don't really know, I just need to start my life and living it better. But now I have a different view. I know that I'm going to party when I get out and then I'm going to take computers.

MVL: Was jale worth it?

Lazy: My jale took three minutes and now I'm doing seven months. Three minutes cost me seven months and it's not worth it.

Hillcrest Juvenile Hall

MVL: Grandpa, you were facing 25 years to life. How did you feel at the time?

Grandpa: It hit me real hard. I felt like escaping. Then I went to my room to think about how big I would get and I realized that I would not see my family and not have my freedom and from now on, I had to knock on the door just to go take a piss.

MVL: Any advice for the "Brown-n-Proud" out there?

Grandpa: When you are behind the trigger, take a good look at your target and ask yourself, "Do I really want to take down one of our warriors?"

MVL: What about the chavalitos that think killing our own is cool?

Grandpa: The white man is out there wishing for you to commit a crime against our own people so that he can take two Raza out with one stone. The one who commits the crime gets 25 years and the victim is dead. The gavacho, the white man, stands happy holding the money.

MVL: I sincerely hope that when you guys get out, you keep educating your minds so we, the "Brown-n-Proud," can rise up politically, socially and economically. Our destiny is to regain our stolen land from the foreign gavacho.

Raza Day at Stanford University

MVL: Why did Raza from Stanford University organize Raza Day, and what is it all about?

Carmella: We realized that we are in a position to inspire the youth because we made it academically. We have tremendous financial resources coming from the university and all of our heart lies at home. We want to help those that are in the same position we were in four years ago.

MVL: Even though most politicians are being controlled by special interests, I still think that it's our duty to vote, 'cause one day we will have a strong brown voice in the political arena. With that in mind, why do you think Raza should vote?

Adam: We should vote to take over this system so that we can put our system back in place.

Titi and Angel: So we could put a piece of our mind into what we feel and want.

Sandra: Just like white people have the right, we have the right too.

Janae: California's population is mainly Raza and we don't have any politicians that are Chicanos.

Mayra: We go to school here and we work here, this is our home. Everything the Caucasians do, like their laws and regulations, affects us in every way, so we should have a say.

Lizet: Because we are reaching to be the majority and we should have our say because things affect us. La realidades es que la majoria de la Raza que a estado aquí más de diez anos y no se asen cuidados y por eso mos pushan around.

MVL: Simon, gente que acerse cuidadanos para que logramos a quitar estas leyes injustas contra nuestra linda Raza. Y con respecto Lizet, nosotros la Raza have always been and always will be the majority in Califas and the whole content of "America" because

this is our land spiritually, morally and historically. We just need to get ourselves organized and become a great political voice for the "Brown-n-Proud."

Latin Youth Summit

The Latino Youth Summit had several speakers and workshops to help educate La Raza. Proposition 209 is gonna damage education. Gavachos will come up with any excuse so we won't get hired. We should start organizing and start voting to take back our rights.

MVL: What did you learn from the speakers?
Raza: We should stick together and better ourselves. Pete Wilson is getting rid of Affirmative Action, so it's all about organizing the people to vote. If students could sign papers to get rid of a bad principal, then we should do the same thing to Pete Wilson, because he is a bad governor.
– I'm proud of our Raza porque ya sabemos lo que somos...Unidad.
– It's cool that people actually want to unite, so there is still hope for our people.

Mr. Goofy: They were talking about our Raza, that we should stop killing our own people, because the white fuckers are laughing at us and are saying that we are stupid, no-good wetbacks. Another vato said that we should unite and fight for our gente, brown dignity and to stay strong.

La Virgen de San Juan de los Lagos Jalisco is the Milagro for Watsonville's Violence

For the last few months, a few vatos have been found dead. One vato was found dead in the rio. Also, cowardly acts have been per-

formed—a drive-by was done, leaving a 16-year-old dead; a little girl of nine was also killed. So, abuelitos, hijas, tíos, madres y padres attended a máss hoping to stop the violence.

LA FAMILIA COUNSELING SERVICES, HAYWARD

Ruben Rodriguez brought the Virgen to help out with the violence in this town and to thank God for the success she brought to the Rodriguez family. The family all worked in the fields and Grandpa is thankful because they are all successful. There are 18 grandchildren and every one is going to college; some are already in college.

The family is asking the Virgen to help them out in the community. Que no hagan tanta violencia. Que pare la violencia y la gente sea más unida.

National Peace Summit, in Santa Cruz

Nane Alejandrez, Santa Cruz, Califas: When I think of nonviolence, I look back to our teacher César Chávez. This is dedicated to him. He left us with a spirit, "Que si se puede." We must organize to stop the madness so that our children can survive.

Blanca Martinez, Dallas, Tejas: It breaks my heart to see the pain in our people. There is high gang violence and drug addiction, and I have cried to God to help my people. We are here to create some solutions so we can tell our carnalitos, "Hey, I feel your pain... I have been there." Together we have strength. Homeboys are all about love and we must heal our hearts. My oldest son got shot while protecting two guys. My street nature came out that I must kill them, but then I realized and asked God to forgive me and forgive the guy who shot my son. We need to practice what we preach and work together. We must put away the chismes, backstabbing y

HOMIES AT THE
NATIONAL PEACE
SUMMIT

la envidia. We must be aware of all that and help each other. We are hurting ourselves with that in mind, traigan la paz a sus barrios.

MVL: Como le estan gustando la conferencia?

Chicago: Todavia hay esperanza para terminar la violencia en los barrios. Tambien la cultura nos ayuda a entender más de nuestra gente de diferentes estados.

Coming to Santa Cruz, California was a very beautiful experience because I have learned más que antes de mi cultura y me Raza.

Homer Leija, Fresnal Barrios Unidos: 187 got designed for those who can't stay here. 184 is for those who can stay here but will end up in prison. Affirmative Actíon has been dismantled, and we must get involved politically to stop this. It takes four years to set up in colleges, but only three months in jails, so we are a big business for the jail system.

Luis J. Rodriguez, Author of *Always Running*: Drugs and alcohol are selfish. All you care about is your next fix and you forget about your kids. We need programs that keep people off drugs and give them something to live for. Our kids are forced to fail and are directed to prison. The politicians built prisons to house our kids, they are being set up for prison. The original barrios were there to protect gente. Now there is no healing going on. We need to tell our stories, even though wounds will open. Language is power. That is why they took away our language and taught us bad English. They beat our language out of us. When you are giving your history, you are giving your future.

Frank, East Los, Califas: I'm from East Los, Primera Flats and my barrio was my only existence. I never graduated from high school but I went to college and graduated. I started teaching school and overheard a gavacho say, "Them wetbacks must stay away from here." Then I realized that I should go back to the barrio and teach. I felt a connectíon to Nicaragua so I joined the revolucion. I was teaching young kids Chicano Studies in Chinandega, but they stopped coming to school because they went to fight in the revolucion. They used to say, "Patria Libre o Morir!" So I went to join them. There were many Chicanos in Nicaragua fighting for La Revolucion, and that experience has made me see that we have no borders and that we are one people.

"El Movimiento" Workshop: Who are Norteños/Sureños? They are Raza and we all have a role to play in the movimiento. Make an effort in communicating with one another. The movement is what La Raza sacrifices for in the barrio. It's going to take sacrifice to forgive a carnal. It's going to take sacrifice to put down the cuete. There's hope when the young get involved. We focus on topics that affect Raza. We get gente to register to vote. Society quiere que nos matemos. There's nothing wrong in wearing our baggy pants, but when they see us they always think negative and look at us as if we don't belong here. So I joined the Brown Berets to help my people. The Europeans don't want us to know our heroes, so we wouldn't get pissed off at what they have done to us. Take a look at what's happening around you. Get involved and make a difference!

Rudy de Victory Temple, El Paso, Tejas

MVL: What are some alternatives to loqueras?
Rudy: Boxing, basketball. But to see change, that comes through the gospel, having a relatíonship with Jesus. Cristo es lo que te cambia.

MVL: Como has cambiado?
Rudy: I don't gangbang. Now I can love that homeboy that I was once against. We get to save and help them out. We make ourselves available for the kids in the barrio.

MVL: How could you guys empower the gente in the barrio politically, economically and socially?
Rudy: Politically by showing our Raza that we are more than the old stereotype. We have shown our people that they can better themselves with Christ and be whatever they want.

Financially we are struggling and we depend on God. We raise funds to help out the barrios and as long as we are with Christ, we can become President of the United States.

Socially we show the Raza to love each other and encourage them not to kill over the streets. I forgave a vato who was involved in a drive-by that killed my primo. We bring different vatos from different gangs and we work together. Guys that normally kill each other are now crying with each other and don't trip on what barrio they are from.

LATINO
YOUTH SUMMIT

La Familia Counseling Service, Hayward

MVL: What type of work do you ladies and gentlemen do at La Familia Counseling Service?

La Familia: There are two components; one is called ALMA (Alliance of Latino Mentors Against AIDS). In ALMA we do contact sheets where we interview and do presentations on how AIDS is transmitted and how to prevent it.

MVL: Could you please give the "Brown-n-Proud" clecha on the subject?

ALMA: Transmission comes through unsafe sex (oral, anal and vaginal); it can be passed from mother to baby or through infected needles (IV drug use or simply a tattoo). Before 1985, AIDS could be transmitted through a blood transfusion, because the blood was not screened. Now this is rare.

Prevention comes through abstinence (no sex and no needles), using protection (condoms and dental condoms for oral sex) and not sharing needles. You can sterilize needles by injecting bleach through the needle three times and then rinsing the needle with water three times through.

MVL: Gracias for this life-v saving info. So you gente out there be trucha porque la SIDA esta peligrosa.

La Familia: The second component we offer is the Youth Leadership Program. We go to junior high schools to educate the young on how to succeed and do one-on-one and group consultation.

MVL: Could you run down some of your problem solving situations?

La Familia: There were two Raza groups that didn't get along in school because one group spoke Spanish and the other English. So we taught these kids cultura and their eyes were opened. They realized they shouldn't fight with one another.

MVL: Es sierto que la cultura cura, so it must remain alive and be instilled into our gente. All you Raza out there that think you are better than those who don't speak English, just think for a minute on the following: Our heroes, Pancho Villa, Sandino, Zapata and Che spoke Spanish and fought for our land and our rights against the gavachos. The gavas feared them! Now, we must all learn both languages and use the knowledge to get ahead and preserve our ways. Gente, the majority of "America" speaks Spanish. We are the majority! The gavas know this and they don't want you to realize the "brown side" of things. Asi que no sean pendejos, agarren la onda que somos Raza! The gavas fear us and when we speak Spanish, they don't know what we are thinking. Entienden!?

La Familia: Another problem-solving situation was at Los Cerros Juvenile Hall. We did a group session there for three months about the Norte y Sur. They were there to create hell, so when we got there we told them to respect us and to respect one another. Re-

RUDY DE VICTORY
TEMPLE, EL PASO,v
TEJAS

spect was the number one rule. We got respect and talked about La Cultura, Aztlan. We talked about the different gods, etc. We used cultura to open up their eyes. We helped them set goals. Eventually everyone was cool and began to tolerate each other.

MVL: That's firme. Remember gente, que La Cultura Cura and it must be preserved! Combine our rich past with today's technology and bring back those that are lost in the white and black world. The "brown side" is the only way for La Raza!

Conferencia de Maestros en San Diego

MVL: Why have you chosen teaching as a profession?
Margie: Being a Mechista, I saw the necessity. Chicanos need to be part of the classroom. I was part of the walkout and saw that the school system does not find themselves responsible for meeting the needs of Raza. The curriculum teaches the "American Dream," which is not real. So the companeros and myself try to bring the padres and madres out to be part of the school and bring our point of view forward.

HOMIES IN BUSINESS

Ora! Aquí en este capitulo! Is this beauty or what? Having a bi-lin-gual tonque! Pues, soy como soy! The following are interviews of homies with their own businesses. Hopefully, and I do wish from my corazon, the almighty Creator will open up the eyes of all you "Brown-n-Proud" gente out there so that you put your energies and concentration on your goals and dreams to have a better life and encourage the rest of us to do better in life. Y que asi sea!

Oscar Rios, Mayor of Watsonville

I'm from El Salvador and I came to San Francisco in 1961 with my mother, father and siblings. I graduated from Jefferson High School in Daly City. In high school I was confused about who I was because I was taught a distorted history of our land. I grew up during the time of the Vietnam War, the Brown Be-rets and the San Francisco State riots. My friends talked to me about history and Brown Pride.

In 1969 there was a group of Raza called Los Siete who were ac-cused of shooting a police officer. The police bombed one of their houses, killing an innocent Raza woman. Her family were left on the streets. So a group of people, myself included, got organized to help Los Siete get out of jail. Later, it was proven in court that the policeman was killed by his own partner. After this case, I became more politically aware and began helping labor workers organize.

In 1985 I got involved with the Watsonville cannery strike. It was a hard struggle, but we won and now some of our gente have jobs. In 1989 MALDEF won a suit against the city of Watsonville for their violation of voting rights against La Raza. The workers then encouraged me to run for office.

There is a lot of work to be done. I'm trying to get funding for more programs. There is no land or money, but we are in the process

OSCAR RIOS,
MAYOR OF
WATSONVILLE

of getting a youth center and funding for murals to instill pride and unity. I do letters of recommendation too. My door is open for the vatos and homegirls to come in and talk to me. I'm also working to get people educated on our city government. Before, there was a lot of racism and our issues were not dealt with; there were big problems and a lot of people were not involved. Aquí in Watsonville there is a lot of potential in getting people involved so they can control their own destiny. There is a lot of poverty, lack of jobs, demand for housing and drugs just like any other town but I'm working hard to better our situation.

The youth have a lot of pride. We need to work together and stop killing each other.

Carlos "Cookie" Gonzales, Juvenile Parole Officer

I'm a first generation Chicano, born and raised in the Mission, Folsom Park. From the age of 14 to 18, I was a vato in Folsom Park and then I went to college. That was in the mid-'70s. Back then, clickas were made up of gente who lived in that barrio. Vatos took care of their barrio. Chavalitos were able to play on the calles. Viejitos and viejitas were respected and taken care of. They walked without fear. We watched out for each other and nobody stole from their neighbor. We were a big familia. The only time shit would kick off was when vatos from other clickas would come and show disrespect.

Now it's almost like people from all over can come and claim a turf. A guy from a different city can come down and hang out on the street with other guys from other parts of town and form a gang representing that street. Another phenomenon of today's clickas

are the Norteños that were born Sureños. A lot of them were born and raised in the norte but for some reason they claim sur and have never set foot in East Los or San Diego. I feel sorry for those vatos if they get locked up in the pinta because being from San Fran in any pinto's eyes are viewed as Norteños and expected to run with Norteños. If they claim Sur and live in the Norte, the real Sureños are not going to accept them and they are caught in limbo. They'll have to watch their backs from the Norteños and Sureños. Also, the youngsters are packing cuetes, which is dangerous. They don't know the consequences of using a gun. Before the older vatos who had access to cuetes would only use them as a last resort. Back in those days, only putos who could not fight would use cuetes.

One of my homeboys who got out of the gang life by joining the army moved to Santa Rosa after his discharge. He encouraged me to get into college. He was going to college at the time and was the chair of MEChA at Sonoma State. When he found out I was still fucking up, he recruited me and got me into college through EOP. I was reluctant at first because I was having too much fun with the homeboys. But after a few funerals, I had a change of heart and decided to take my homeboy's offer and moved to Santa Rosa. I was reborn when I took Chicano studies and became a Mechista. I realized the importance of working for my gente through community service and recruited young Raza into higher education. After transferring to San Francisco State, I started working for RAP and its various components in the Mission.

My experience at RAP and my college degree have enabled me to get hired as a juvenile probation officer. Working in an institution that traditionally railroaded our young Raza by locking them up, I use my position to make sure Raza gets a fair shake by providing alternatives to incarceration. Raza have been misun-

CARLOS
"COOKIE"
GONZALES,
JUVENILE
PAROLE
OFFICER

derstood by the system because of cultural and language barriers. Because of this, many Raza youth have been sent to YA on their first offence, compared to other ethnic groups who have benefited from speaking the "Man's Tongue." I am here to start the flow of Raza from jail to college.

In my day, if you didn't have your t-shirt, pants and Pendleton creased, you weren't shit! Shoes were shined, hair combed back and shirts folded a certain way when strolling. The firme ranflas were all Chevies bombas, Impalas, Monte Carlos and trokas. We cruised bumper to bumper Friday and Saturday night. Nowadays, nobody even irons their clothes, they have weird-ass haircuts and they show the crack of their culos. Man, what is the world coming to? Damn!

Actresses Ángela Moya y Lupe Ontiveros

Ángela: It's hard being a Chicana and it's getting harder, so we write our own plays for our people. Lupe has fought to get good parts 'cause we get parts like maids and prostitutes.

Lupe: Yes, it's always been hard, but it's also hard for Raza males. We are very supportive with each other. What you saw on stage was because we have known each other for 18 years. We are pissed off because we don't get recognized. We are setting a movement and we are the ones paying the price by getting the bad roles. If Raza don't have role models then our young will have no hope.

The powers that be, producers, the decision makers, don't have any idea who we are as people. They think of us as maids and gardeners and have no respect for us. We must boycott them to hurt their pocketbooks. Their products are the commercials. If we turn off the TV or if we stop watching those piece-of-shit action films that don't include our gente, then we will hurt their pocketbooks.

We have lost faith in ourselves. We need to support Raza film production like *Selena*. Go out and support Raza film!

Sometimes we feel alone. To get accepted to a group we sometimes do things we don't want to do. You don't have to be part of a group that disrespects you as women.

Ángela: We need to take more responsibilities for our actions. We need the four Fs: A que tener FE en ti misma. La FUERZA en ti misma. FRANQUESA con ti misma. y FIRMESA en ti misma.

Oscar Miranda, Second Camera Assistant
Oscar on the set of *Dangerous Minds*

I'm a second camera assistant. My duties are to assist the first camera assistant by making sure we have the right lenses, filters and enough film. We set up the camera shots and I'm in charge of the film count, reloading magazines and I slate every scene. After our shooting, I make sure the film that has been shot gets into the producer's hands so it can be sent to the lab and processed. I also work for Channel 22, a Chicano TV station in Los Angeles. I work as an editor for the four, seven and ten o'clock newscasts. And I am an actor. I was in the TV series *Dangerous Minds*, and played Oscar, a high school gangster who was trying to get out of his gang because he got his hina pregnant. I was also in *High School High*. I played a student who was in a gang. I was in a Chicano TV show called *Placas*, too.

It bothers me that Hollywood stereotypes us and looks at us only as a minority. It makes it hard for our people to get a decent role in the movies. Through my experience I only get gangster roles and it bothers me a bit. Hopefully that will change someday and we Chicanos will get better roles and opportunities in the movie industry.

It all started for me when I lived in Bakersfield, Kalifas. My love for acting and the film industry grew when I saw the film *E.T.* So I left Bakersfield for the big time in Los Angeles y gracias a Dios mi suerte a sido grande. Pero como te dige, I've been in a few movies and TV series. When I arrived in Los Angeles, I started working as a busboy at El Torrito in Burbank to help get me through film school. Then I started applying for work at production companies and my persistence got me hired to Harmony Pictures. From then on, I started getting hired by different producers.

The key is to work well with a producer so they keep hiring you. In this business, you don't know when you'll work again. Hollywood has to know you and what I mean by that is that you have to know enough people in the industry to keep you working. I've paid my dues by working for free to prove that they can trust me on the job.

I hope to make it as an actor someday and be able to help out the underdogs. All my hard work has not been in vain, because I've learned a lot. I would be able to direct my own projects. Presently I'm writing a script with the help of my homies from the Notorious LAC (Lethal Assassins Click). This script is based on the real life story of my carnal y mi camarada Mr. Azteca. I'm also involved in a project which is being directed by Damian Chapa (AKA Miklo from *Bound by Honor*). The movie will be called *The Lonely Life of Downey Hall*, so be on the lookout for it.

To my gente, I just want you to know that working in the entertainment business is not easy, but don't get discouraged, just work hard at it. Que Dios los bendigas.

11.

REAL LIFE HEROES

Qvole readers,

The facts that I'm gonna run down for you will never make it inside the classrooms unless I'm there giving you cats clecha! First of all, European Americans don't have heroes. Unless you people think John Wayne, Sylvester Stallone and Batman and Robin are real. They are simply make-believe. You people don't have any real heroes! Now a few of you might consider people in the armed forces your heroes, but guess what, the majority of people in the armed forces are Chicanos and Latinos from the barrio! Before we got incorporated into "Amerika," we were fighting the Europeans that ventured across the ocean and buried their filthy teeth in the throats of my ancestors' civilization.

My gente's heroes are not a Hollywood creation. Our heroes had heartbeats, with hot blood running through their veins. They fought for the liberty of our lands. They protected defenseless kids from European terrorists. They fought and died honorably. My ancestors had no choice but to fight against the Europeans and European Americans because they killed kids, raped women and stole the land.

Here are a few examples of real-life heroes:

Augusto Cesár Sandino de Nicaragua —Neither the U.S. Marines firepower or the bombs dropped from planes defeated this great hero. He kicked ass during his 12 long years against U.S. invaders.

José Artigas de South America—Fought against the Spaniards and Portuguese because he wanted social, economical and political rights for the ragged gauchos and Native Americans. So he led them to an agrarian revolution for nine years.

Emiliano Zapata de Mexico—Fought for land reform and for the rights of the poor and to correct the wrongs of society.

Reies López Tijerina de Nuevo Mexico—Founded the Alliance Federal de Mercedes in the '60s to search out the return of the lost, sold and stolen land grants that once belonged to La Raza in parts of Arizona, New Mexico and Texas.

Juana Gallo de Mexico—Led men into battle against the corrupt government of Mexico after seeing her father and other villagers hanged for defending their land.

Don Juan N. Cortina de Tejas—From 1859 to 1875, he led vaqueros to occupied Brownsville, Texas and claimed the Republic of the Rio Grande while fighting the white Americans (better known back then as gringos).

Joaquín Murrieta—Came back to California, walked into his cabin while 13 white Americans were raping his young wife. Joaquín fought but was beat until he no longer moved. He lived and took revenge. For years he searched for the 13 white rapists until he found every one of them. Each of the cowards died begging for mercy. The following is a letter from Joaquín Murrieta:

I was once a great admirer of Americans. I thought they were the noblest, most honorable and high-minded people in the world. I had met many in my own country and all forms of tyranny seemed as hateful to them as a rule of the gachupines (Spaniard foreigners) as to the Mexicans. I was sick of the constant wars and insurrections in my native land and I came here thinking I would end my days in California as an American citizen. I located first near Stockton, but I was constantly annoyed and insulted by my neighbors and was not permitted to live in peace. I went then to the placers (gold mines) and was driven from my mining claim. I went into business and was cheated by everyone in whom I trusted. At every turn, I was swindled and robbed by the very men for whom I had the greatest friendship and admiration. I saw the Americans daily in acts of the most outrageous and lawless injustice or of cunning and mean duplicity hateful to every honorable mind.

I then said to myself that I will revenge my wrongs and take the law into my own hands. The Americans who have injured me, I will kill and those who have not, I will rob because they are Americans. My trail shall be red with blood and those who seek me shall die or I shall lose my own life in the struggle! I will not submit tamely to outrage any longer.

I have killed many, I have robbed many and many more will suffer in the same way. I will continue to the end of my life to take vengeance on the race that has wronged me so shamefully.

In contrast to this, besides the Hollywood creation of make-believe heroes for little white kids, greed and money are the real heroes for the unculture, the Anglo-Saxon race and their siblings. In 1935, General Smedley D. Butler, who headed many expeditions for big business, indicated the following:

I spent thirty-three years and four months in active military service... during that period, I spent most of my time being a high class muscle-man for Big Business, for Wall Street and for the Bankers. In short, I was a racketeer, a gangster for capitalism... I helped make Mexico and especially Tampico safe for American oil interests in 1914. I helped make Haiti and Cuba a decent place for the National City Bank boys to collect revenues in... I helped purify Nicaragua for the international banking house of

Brown Brothers in 1909–12. I brought light to the Dominican Republic for American sugar interests in 1916. I helped make Honduras "right" for American fruit companies in 1903.

Greed, money and destruction are your heroes, you little white kid, while the young "Brown-n-Proud" stand tall and strong and say in class that their heroes are human beings with the pulse and blood of warriors fighting for familia, Mother Earth, equality, freedom and human rights.

And now some more stories from my gente's heroes.

Tiburcio Vasquez
From *Drink Cultura* by Jose A. Burciaga

Young Tiburcio lived and witnessed the gavacho invasion of California. He came from a distinguished family and was born in California when it was part of Mexico. From childhood to his teens, he watched the gavacho invasion and saw his gente reduced to second-class citizens and worse.

In 1850, when Tiburcio was 15 years old, California was admitted into the Union and the Foreign Miners Tax severely penalized anyone who was Raza while gavachos got rich without paying high (or any) tax at all. Que gacho 'cause it was Raza that taught gavachos how to pan for gold.

By 1856, much of the land had changed to gavacho ownership through armed confrontations, legislations and swindles. Raza were robbed of their land. Hangings of Mexicanos became so common during the 1840s and 1850s that newspapers didn't even bother reporting them. Californios who resisted the invading gavachos became outlaws, although many Mexicanos considered them heroes. Professor Rodolfo Acuna, a California Chicano history professor, and author of *Occupied America*, wrote:

Resistance also manifested itself in anti-social behavior. When the colonized cannot earn a living within the system, or when they are degraded, they strike out. The most physical way is to rebel. This can be done in an organized way as expressed by Juan Cortina in Texas, or it can express itself in bandit activity. An analysis of the life of Tiburcio Vasquez clearly demonstrates that.

Major Benjamin Truman, editor of the *Los Angeles Star*, interviewed Tiburcio Vasquez some 22 years after his first alleged crime. This is Vasquez's own perspective:

My career grew out of the circumstances by which I was surrounded. As I grew into manhood, I was in the habit of attending balls and parties given by the Native Californians into which the Americans (who were growing in population) would force themselves. They would shove native born men aside, monopolizing the dance and the women. This was around 1852. A spirit of hatred and revenge took possession of me. I had numerous fights in defense of what I believed to be my rights and those of my countrymen. I believed we were unjustly and wrongfully deprived of the social rights that belonged to us. So perpetually was I involved in these difficulties, that at length I determined to leave the thickly settled portions of this country and did so.

Tiburcio resented the gavacho sailors that swarmed over Monterey. He became preoccupied with watching over his two sisters, guarding them against the aggressive and crude ways of foreign Anglo-American culture. His first serious run-in with the law occurred in 1852, when he attended a dance with his friend Anastacio Garcia who was married to Tiburcio's cousin, Guadalupe Gomez. At the dance, Antonia Romero was dancing to a song, a favorite dance in which the men tossed their hats on the women they liked as they danced by them. One young gavacho sailor decided to place his hat onto Antonia Romero's head instead of flinging it and a fight broke out (differing cultural customs can mean everything in such situations. The perfectly accepted gavacho custom of "cutting in" was an insult to a Californio). After the fight ensued, Constable Hardmount was called in to quell the tension. When he appeared

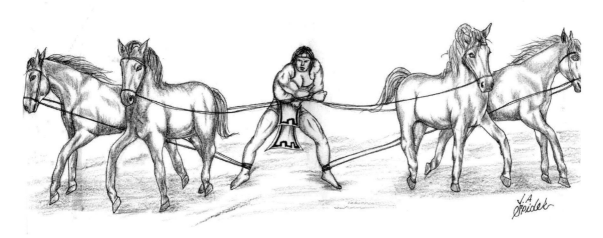

on the scene and began to question the people, someone turned off the lights. By the time they were back on, the constable was dead. Jose Guerra, Anastacio Garcia and Tiburcio Vasquez were accused of the crime.

TUPAC AMARU
BY VICTOR A.
SPIDER

Jose Guerra was lynched the morning after the murder without trial. Vasquez and Garcia escaped but a few months later. Garcia was apprehended in Los Angeles and returned to Monterey for a trial. But the trial never took place, because outraged vigilantes found out and raided the jail. Garcia was immediately lynched. Tiburcio Vasquez did what any Californio of that time would have done under the circumstance s. Because due process in an Anglo-American court of justice seemed impossible, he decided that it would be better to live outside gavacho law. It would have been suicide to do otherwise. Vasquez went to his mother and told her he had decided to start a different life.

"I asked her for and obtained her blessing and at once, commenced a career as a robber."

He further stated,

"I had confederates with me from the start and I was always recognized as a leader."

His fast-paced life and numerous robberies took a halt when he was arrested in 1858 for stealing a horse in Los Angeles. He was sent to San Quentin. In 1859, Vasquez participated in a prison break but was soon captured. In prison he was active in stirring up revolts among the inmates. Released in 1863, Tiburcio resumed his former life. Despite intense and costly searches across the state, Vasquez always eluded capture:

All of these Mexicans are his friends. They offer him the shelter of their homes and when he is pursued they tell the officers the most prodigious lies without any compunction. He has no band or gang unless the entire Mexican population of the mountain regions of Fresno, Tulare, Monterey and Los Angeles can be called such.

In all of these countries, Vasquez could count on the moral and physical support of his countrymen and countrywomen. Despite his general support among the Spanish-speaking populace, he was not without Californio enemies. Such was the case with Abdon's wife, Rosaria. Abdon supposedly discovered them in flagrante delicto and aided in the capture of Tiburcio. Otherwise Vasquez was prudent, intelligent, resourceful and commanding. Many times when traveling, he would have one companion ride far ahead of him and another far behind, to warn him of any danger. When camping, Tiburcio normally chose to sleep away from the main campsite. Another favored tactic, when holding up a stagecoach, was for Tiburcio and his men to form a single-file line on horseback so as to appear as one horseman to the stagecoach drivers. At the last moment, they would spread out and surprise their intended prey. According to Stanford University history professor Albert Camarillo, "Vasquez created fear in the Anglos because of his revolutionary potential. Tiburcio, on at least one occasion, had ambitions of effecting an uprising or revolution against the Yankee invaders of California."

Indeed Tiburcio Vasquez was able to free himself of the gavacho colonization and became a quasi-bandit revolutionary. In fact, to the end Vasquez had hoped that before hanging he would have a chance to make a speech on the scaffold, calling for a revolution regardless of the great numbers and dominance of the gavacho invaders.

Tiburcio Vasquez was eventually captured after he was betrayed by Abdon Leiva in a secret operation. Following a lengthy trial and much publicity, Vasquez was hanged at 30 minutes past one on the afternoon of March 19, 1875. Fourteen minutes later he was declared dead.

Tupac Amaru
From *Open Veins of Latin America*
by Eduardo Galeano

La Conquista destroyed the foundations of our ancient civilizations. The Españoles were gold-hungry, and our gente were forced to become slaves to bring out the golden rock from the mines. Indio sculptors, architects, engineers, astronomers and farmers were sent into the mines to make others rich.

In 1781, Tupac Amaru, a mestizo chief and a direct descendant of the Inca emperors started a rebellion against the forced labor mines. Tupac Amaru rode into the plaza of Tungasuca, sentenced the royal corregidor Antonio Juan de Arriaga to death and announced the liberty for his gente from the mines of Potosi Mita, Peru. Thousands of mestizos and Indios joined Tupac Amaru and fought for their liberty. Tupac ended the taxes and

I, Rigoberta Menchú

AN INDIAN WOMAN IN GUATEMALA

RIGOBERTA
MENCHÚ DE
GUATEMALA

forced labor. Victories and defeat followed and at the end, Tupac was betrayed and captured by his own chiefs. Tupac was handed over in chains to the royalists. The Examiner Areche entered Tupac's cell and asked the names of his followers. Tupac Amaru replied, "There are no other followers here other than you and I. You as oppressor and I as liberator deserve to die."

Later, Tupac was tortured along with his wife, chavalitos and chief aides in Cuzco's plaza del Wacaypata. Tupac's tongue was cut out. His arms and legs were tied to four horses with the intent of quartering him, but his body would not break. Later, he was sent to the gallows where his head was cut. His head, arms and legs were sent to different places. The torso was burned and the ashes thrown in the Rio Watanay. Before his head was cut, he said, "Campesino, your poverty shall no longer feed the máster." Tupac's spirit lies in our corazon as well as the rest of our heroes. Raza, look around you and see how the foreign gavacho is disrespecting our gente.

Rigoberta Menchú de Guatemala by Rosa M.

In our cultura we have many heroes, but where are the heroines? Why aren't they equally represented? I know that there are many Raza heroines and Rigoberta is one of them. Not many people know who she was and what she went through.

Rigoberta is an indigenous female from Guatemala. She comes from the Quiche people. Like many Raza, she was put through hell and back by the government—but like many Raza females, she still stands strong. Rigoberta worked in the fields since she was a young girl, where she was exploited by landowners. Rigoberta's parents were the community leaders there. She had organizing skills and began to organize her community. She was fed up with all the wrong that her people were enduring, so she and her family were helping to organize communities. That is when trouble came her way. The landowners weren't too happy about the idea that these people would want more rights, so they decided to bring in the government. Soon the army were camping out in people's villages, waiting for an opportunity to mássacre. Rigoberta endured a lot of pain. During this time she lost two brothers and her parents.

Rigoberta's two-year-old brother died of malnutrition and her other brother was kidnapped, beaten and tortured. The army tied him up including his testicles and forced him to run, and they threw him in a muddy well with rotten corpses. He was tortured for 16 days. They cut his fingers off, burned and cut parts of his skin and shaved his head so they could cut his head and pull the skin down on either side. Later, the villages were forced to attend a "show" and were told that if they failed to attend, they would be killed immediately. When everyone arrived, officers lined up the tortured people who had cuts all over their bodies. These people were swollen and half dead with their clothes damp from the oozing liquid coming out of them. There was a female in the line with her private parts shaved and one nipple of her breast was missing. Her other breast was cut off. All the tortured had their tongues cut off or split apart. The officers were ordered to pour gasoline on the still alive bodies.

After her brother was murdered, Rigoberta's father went off to organize and join the guerillas. He and some compañeros occupied the Spanish embassy in protest of the inhumane way they were being treated. He and the other men were killed by a bomb that hit the embassy. Rigoberta kept working to organize her people. Soon after, her mother was kidnapped, tortured and raped. After three days, her ears were cut off along with bits of her body. As she was dying, they continually beat and raped her. After she was dead, soldiers urinated inside her mouth and let animals eat her corpse.

Rigoberta soon got word that the soldiers were looking for her. Families would let her hide in their homes, but she soon grew weary of putting these innocent people in danger. So with the help of her compañeros, she fled to Mexico where she began to speak on the lifestyle of indigenous people and the injustices her people had to endure. Many people offered to help her, and after the army calmed, she returned to Guatemala. She returned because she was a leader

CHE

and a child of the cause. She is still alive today, because the cause gives her strength. Rigoberta understands the risk to her life by returning, but she is willing to die for what she loves.

Rigoberta Menchú is only one example of the many heroines we have as mujeres. If you are looking for another one, look into a mirror. We too have resisted for more than 500 years, and we are still alive and going strong. Whether we are soldiers of the streets or de la Causa, we must fight for La Raza and stop fighting each other.

Mujeres, stand strong, because we are the Mothers of this Earth. We must take care of it and keep it alive. Que viva la mujer!!!

The Significance of September 15 and 16 by FIG

On September 16, 1810, in Dolores, Mexico, the cry of revolt was given—"Grito de Dolores"—by Miguel Hidalgo, a parish priest and the leader of the movement. He led an army of Indian parishioners to battle against the Spanish troops who were loyal to Spain. He was captured and executed in 1811, and the leadership was taken over by another priest, José Maria Morelos, who continued the movement that Hidalgo began. Morelos did not give in to the pressure of the Spanish troops until 1815, when he was captured and executed. Between 1815 and 1821, the movement degenerated into sporadic guerrilla activity with Vicente Guerrero as the leader of this struggle during these years of hide-and-seek. By 1812, the liberals and conservatives agreed to join forces for independence by adhering to the plan de Iguala, known as the "Union de Peninsulares." By the summer of 1821, nearly all of Mexico rallied to the plan. We celebrate September 16 to remind us of our ancestors and heritage, and to feel proud of what we accomplished. The spirit that they had, we still carry in our hearts. Que viva la causa!

The Spanish colonial rule in Nicaragua, Guatemela, Honduras, El Salvador and Costa Rica came to an end on September 15, 1821. The gente congratulated their triumph with a big celebration at the Palacio de los Capitanes Generales in Guatemala City. Some of the heroes were Máximo Jerez from Nicaragua, Pedro Molina from Guatemala, José Matías Delgado from El Salvador, Juan Santamaria from Costa Rica and Francisco Morazán from Honduras. Carnalas y carnales unidos we will control totally, it's been done in the past. Let's wake up the Raza and identify the real enemy—the corrupted politicians and crooked officials who want us dead. Just look at their politics and the way it affects our people. Unidos rifaremos total. Hasta la victoria!

César Chávez

From a pachuco to a great Raza leader, César Chávez is a great role model for all of us to be proud of. He grew up in the barrio as a pachuco and worked in the fields. As a young man he experienced the injustice that the gavacho landowners did and are doing to our people. César Chávez devoted his life to organize farm workers into a union for better working conditions in the fields. Before Chávez, the farmers were paid about $1 an hour for 10 to 12 hours of work. They didn't have a place to stay, so they slept outside in the fields. At times they didn't even have running water, so they suffered under the blazing sun. Those who didn't have papers were deported on payday, so they never got paid. Harsh chemicals were sprayed on the fields and often the Raza would die from them or give birth to deformed babies. This is still happening! Safeway sells chemically infected grapes that are killing the Raza who pick them. Consumer health is at stake!

Chávez's life had gone from one struggle to another. His house was taken away and he was beaten and sent to jail for standing against greedy landowners, police and politicians who were getting over on our people. Regardless of those powerful enemies, César Chávez kept fighting for our gente's rights in the fields. They never sold out and never quit! With the help of Dolores Huerta and many Raza, Chávez boycotted, protested and demanded better wages, housing, safety unions and tu sabes just the basics like food on the table and a roof over one's head in our own land. But Pete Wilson, the governor of Califas, and landowners did everything in their power so our people would remain voiceless and oppressed in the fields.

To all you locas and locos, one of us can make a difference. César Chávez made a difference and his name will shine into the cosmic world along with Sandino, Zapata, Villa, Che, Murieta and many others. César Chávez helped our people and a lot of our people have come into the United Farm Workers union to continue the struggle for the betterment of the farmer. Viva César Chávez. Hasta la victoria!

TRUE STORIES
FROM THE BARRIOS

The following are true stories from different barrios throughout Califas, Aztlan.

Clown Face
By Lagrima R.R.

Sometimes when I would look into his eyes I'd see my reflection. I'd wonder if it's me he sees. How those eyes laughed at me so many times and how my eyes ached from the endless lagrimás.

When Juan was sent to the state pen for possession of cocaine, I promised him I would wait day and night for him. But there was something I couldn't understand; every time I would go down to see him he would refuse to see me. So many nights I would cry wondering what I did wrong. He was a part of me I could not let go of... el sol, el silencio, the happiness and the sadness. He stole my innocence and I stole his. We were so lucky to find one another, but then he found an otro amor. A love that was really hate. A love that killed and stole. This love was his gang, his clicka. He grew passionate for his barrio, to protect and gain their respect. Pretty soon I was watching our love slowly dying out... como una rose dies without her water. I soon found out that he was more in love with his gang than with his own ruca.

He was sentenced to five years and for five years I was punished to live this vida without touching him, kissing him or looking into his dark brown eyes, punished to be alone. So many noches I would cry for him, resando to diosito to give him one more chance to change his ways. I could, I would change him.

After about four years of suffering depression, I received a letter from him. My heart sank when I saw that it was from him. My hands began to shake as I opened the letter. As I read the words the tears would fall endlessly from relief. Every sentence filled me with such felizidad. Every word was like poetry. I read...

Me Querida Chiquita,

Someone once told me that love makes a man weak and therefore I would not love. During the past years, I have had time to think, to learn life and what it is all about. I have learned how much I have hurt you but I too was hurting. Tu sabes that I have treated you like a piece of shit. To this day I still wonder why you stayed by my side? Pero sabes Angelica, I learned in this pinche pinta that love, el amor, is what keeps a man living y un hombre de verdad ain't afraid to show it to his ruca. Por eso, I hope you can forgive me. Please te pido perdon.

Love por siempre hasta la eternidad.

I stared at the letter feeling confusion; feeling happy but sad, and then so angry. All I could do was cry.

The following day, I went to visit him. As I sat and waited for his presence, I began to remember when we were 14 years old y el me dijo:

"Sabes que Chiquita? Siempre te voy a querer no matter what happens. I will always protect you como una rosa hecho de cristal so delicate and fragile."

I can remember that so clearly. The years, how they've past, and now I am sitting here in this room for criminals.

The door finally opened and interrupted my thoughts. Slowly I lifted my eyes. I lost my breath to see his face again. I forced a smile to swallow my tears. Luego he picked up his phone, and I did too. There was silence and hesitation. I wanted to say something, anything, pero que? Finally he broke the silence...

"Your eyes tell me sadness, have I done this to you?"

His face looked old and tired. His eyes were filled with guilt and sadness. I couldn't find the words I wanted to say, so I just looked away.

"Sabes Angel?" he said. "They might let me out early on good behavior. When I get out, I promise I will make it up to you."

One year went by quickly and through his letters he showed me how much he had changed and everything was going to be how it was. When he came home, it was like being born again. I felt as if a strange fuerza took over mi cuerpo. To be in his arms was like a sueño come true for me. One month after, I found out I was carrying his baby. He was so feliz cuando le dije. Huvieras visto how proud he was. But this sueño soon became a nightmare all over again. Unfortunately the Juan I thought I knew became a man of weakness and disgrace, not only to me but to his baby.

Juan would fall into deep depression and instead of turning to me to talk, he turned to alcohol. He would become so helpless. And he would come home todo borracho and cry to me how his life was fucked up and how hard it was for him to grow up in los barrios. I would have to remind him that he had to stop his drinking porque he had to be a good role model for his hijo. So many nights he would promise to stop and so many nights he would return to me in tears. Five months pregnant and I was the one who had to take care of him when he couldn't even walk straight. I was the one who had to drag him inside when he couldn't make it to the door. I would never lose hope for him to change. I wanted us to be a familia so bad. A

ILLUSTRATION BY
VICTOR A. SPIDER

familia that neither me or Juan had.

When my baby nasio, Juan had just left to a party in the city. I was scared and I hated when Juan left me alone. Esa noche le dije to please stay home because I was not feeling muy bien. Pero he told me, "Look, it ain't my fucking problem that you got your ass pregnant!" And with those terrible words, he grabbed the puerta and I grabbed his arm.

"Por favor Juan, no me dejes asi," I begged him.

He pushed me away and opened the door. As I tried to give one last attempt to ask him to stay, he slammed the door with such fury that I didn't realize that he slammed it on my hand. The pulsating pain of my fingers being crushed made me scream a horrible cry. "Maldito seas!" The door swung open and I fell to the floor looking up at his enraged face.

"No me mortifiques más chiquita!"

To be honest I can't remember much more. All I know is that I awoke in a hospital and on that sad and lonely night where everyone was a stranger to me, I gave birth to a beautiful baby girl. She has been my only source of happiness since. I named her Alegria.

A month passed, and then another, without hearing una palabra from him. When I hold her in my arms, I see her daddy's eyes looking back at me. What am I going to tell her when she asks me where her daddy is?

"Hijita, te prometo que te voy a querer para siempre. Te voy a darte lo mejor. I promise I will fight for you. I will make you stronger than me. I will teach you my mistakes so you can learn not to be a clown como tu mamás."

I remember one time cuando el cielo se olvido de respirar, cuando las estrellas se olvidaron de reflejar sobre la tierra. I was awakened by a loud heavy pounding at my door. My baby woke up from her sound sleep and I took her in my arms. I walked over to the door and took a glance out into the oscuridad only to find a shadow with no name. It was too dark to see who it might have been so I asked, "Quien es?" There was silence but soon I heard a low moan.

"Chiquita... dejame entrar."

My heart se me cayo al suelo. I held my baby closer and stayed silent.

"Chiquita!"

Alegria began to cry.

"Mi hijita please don't cry... please." I kept whispering.

"Let me in Angelica! I know you are there, I hear my baby!"

Then tears began to fall from my eyes. I began to pray, "Diosito deme fuerza." He began to beg in a low tired tone.

"Por favor dejame ver mi bebe."

When he said those words I felt great pain in my heart. I knew I had to stay strong and not let him hurt me like he had done in the past.

"Vete dejame dejame en paz! Eres una mala sombra en mi vida!"

My heart wanted to scream, "Please stay with us because we need you." I heard something break in the kitchen. My baby was startled by the sharp shatter. I ran to the kitchen.

"Juan estas loco?"

He had broken the window on the door to unlock it. He walked toward me staring at his hijita.

"Juan, I'm warning you."

"Mira, I know... I know I have fucked up in the past but please don't take mi propio hijo away from su propia sangre."

"She is not tu hija. You can't just come and claim this baby as yours! Where were you all this time? Where were you when I needed you, Juan?" I burst into tears, feeling so tired of always putting on a smiling face when I was crying on the inside, tired of telling la gente que estoy bien cuando en realidad me siento mal.

"Sabes que Juan? Vete al diablo y sabes what else? You are nothing to me anymore and God forbid if you will ever be anything to my baby."

"No Angel te lo suplico." He fell to his knees. "I have no one."

His face, I won't ever forget the way it looked. It expressed pain and hurt and the tears, how they kept falling down his worn-out face.

"Give me one more chance te lo juro por Dios I will change."

To see his tears fall endlessly from his eyes broke my heart apart. How much he has put me through and how many times he has made me cry. But even though he had hurt me, my love for him hasn't died. I wanted to run to him and tell him how much I wanted him to take me into his arms and tell me that he still loves me. It was pure torture to see his pain. In my heart I felt the same. I couldn't take his torture anymore. The tears that fell from my eyes felt like hot blood dripping from the wounds that his thorns had punctured in my tender heart. He reached out slowly with his hands, scared of what my reaction might be. The tears had given him permission to touch my face.

"Te amo Angelica."

I tried to resist him but it was like all my passion that I have felt for him took over my body, and before I knew it we were in each other's arms.

Esa noche he held his baby for the very first time. As the time passed, I learned to forgive, but never forgot. Alegria grew to be his main happiness. It would seem to me that the only time I would see him smile or laugh was when he'd hold his little hijita. Sometimes I would feel celosa. I would have to share his love con otra persona, but I know that's selfish of me.

Todos los dias I would wonder how much longer is this dream going to last. I would watch him sleep and wonder if it was me that made his corazon beat like that. Cerre los ojos y reze en silencio. I just lay there thinking, listening, watching the shadows dance on the wall. As I was about to fall asleep, algo me llamo la atencion. I stared at it in disbelief. I raised my head to take a better look... no, I could not believe what I was seeing. There on his chest was a tatuaje acabado de hacer! It was the face of the devil himself and right on top it read, "Barrio Locos." I lay back down and stared at the ceiling. The tears would drip off the sides of my face. "Pero como puede ser que se metío en esos problemás?" Why now, when everything was getting to be better? Dios mio, he has a familia now to take care of. So many questíons.

The next morning I was dandole de comer a mi hijacuando entro Juan. I was so furious at him I didn't even want to look at his face.

"What the fuck happened to your eyes?"

I ignored his comment and proceeded to feed Alegria.

"Hey Angelica, no me oiste... what happened?"

"Si si te oi!" I threw the bottle on the floor. My eyes were so swollen from crying the night before. Se asusto de ver a me cara.

"Pero que te pasa Angelica?" He backed away from me.

I could read in his eyes, he knew why I was so mad.

"Juan, how could you do this to us? Don't you know you have a family to take care of?" I was yelling at him but it was as if he wasn't listening to a word I was saying. He just sat down and buried his head into his hands. My anger grew into a great passion of hatred.

"Why do you bring yourself into these problemás? You bring us down with you!"

"Ya Angelica! Sabes que Chiquita ya me enfadastes con todos tus chingaderas!"

"Sabes que Juan? You are nothing but a failure; you don't deserve to be called a man. You are a little boy trapped in a man's body. You think you are Mr. Chingon, kicking back with your little barrio. Willing to take out another vato's life at your homies' say-so! That makes you an hombre? What kind of a man are you if you can't even take care of your daughter?"

Right there and then I realized that Juan had just lost the little patience he had left inside him. He rose from the table and without hesitatíon he lifted his right hand across his left shoulder. I closed my eyes for I could see what was coming. I felt the burn of his hard knuckles crash across my face. I lost my balance and fell across the kitchen table where I reached for a glass vase, and without thinking I grabbed it and with all my strength threw it at him. He ducked and it shattered into pieces on the wall. I picked up Alegria who at this time was in a hysterical rage.

"I'm getting the fuck out of here!" I yelled.

So I reached for the door and he grabbed my arm.

"Dejame!" I demanded.

"You can't just leave me, you need me. Where are you going to go? You don't have nobody but me, mi hija," Juan said.

"Sabes que Juan, I can't take this shit any more. I'd rather be alone than be with a chavalo who disrespects his own familia. So let me go and don't worry about me any more. I'll find my way."

Juan began to laugh. "You're forgetting I bring the money, put the food on the table and I am the one who puts the clothes on that baby, you stuck con migo. Welfare won't give you nothing. Pues Angelica, que vas hacer? No house? No work? Aye, and don't forget the baby."

I stared at him in disbelief. My tears, to him didn't mean a thing. He ignored them. I felt trapped. He was right; I had no education, no family, no nothing. He knew he had won, but I couldn't let my pride go down.

"Juan, why don't you take my sight out of your eyes and take my voice from your ears and let me go? I thought you loved me, pues lla se la verdad." I stayed strong and headed out the door.

"Angelica!" He demanded.

I ignored his voice and kept walking.

"Angelica!" he said in a panic.

When he realized I wasn't joking, he ran to me and took Alegria from my arms.

"You're not going anywhere."

With those words he turned around and took her back inside. Por diaz Juan, no me podia mirar la cara. He had no courage.

"Juan, porque no llevamos Alegria al parque? Nunca salimos como una familia. Se me quedo viendo pensativamente. Vamos pues."

So there we were, a familia. How Alegria loved her daddy, and I was a proud lady. Soon I began to notice the expression on Juan's smiling face. Jugando con su hijita changed quickly into a face of uneasiness. He kept wachando los carros pasar por la calle. I could feel something wasn't right. He casually walked over to me and sat down.

"Angelica, the same black car has passed by three times. I need you to act calmada. Go get Alegria, go to the car and stay there."

I turned to him, "Juan por favor, let's just go."

"Do what I tell you, antes que algo te pase."

So I got up and I looked right and then left. My heart began to beat so hard that I could hear it. I picked her up and I slowly walked toward the car. Moving my eyes, scanning the street up and down. Then I looked at Juan, who gave me the look to hurry up. Suddenly everything seemed to be a dream, a horrible dream. I couldn't hear anything but my breath reaching for air. I began to walk faster looking down at my feet and holding Alegria tight.

There it was, coming around the corner, a black Monte Carlo. I began to run, and when I finally reached my car, I struggled hard to open the door. Tenia tanto miedo. Me meti en el carro y I locked all the doors. I buried my face in Alegria's pink and white dress, trying to control my fears. The car stopped behind us and the doors swung open. With no time to waste, cinco vatos se salieron del carro, no mevieron, they were too concentrated on Juan. They all ran toward him. En ese momento me senti como si alguien me huviera sacado el aire. I laid my baby on the floor of the car and covered her con su covejita. I didn't have time to think about what I was doing. All I knew was that I had to help Juan. I swung open the door and ran toward them. Those cowards, those five cowards beating on him with all their strength. Uno de ellos me vio and he ran to me, grabbed me tight and made me watch Juan get punched and kicked and stabbed. I remember screaming and kicking but it was no use, no matter how hard I tried, I could not get away. Cada putaso que le daban era como si me lo dieran a mi. I felt like dying because I was so helpless there was nothing I could do... nothing. There was sangre por todo lado.

"Matame tambien! Matame!" I begged them.

The vato just threw me on the floor and they ran away. I could hear their evil laughs of victory. I crawled over to Juan and rested my head on his bloody chest. I dug my nails into his flesh and cried. I looked up into the sky and asked him "Why?"

"Juan, por favor despiertate!" I grabbed his shirt and tried so hard to wake him.

I touched his face and put my lips on his. I shut my eyes so tight hoping this was a nightmare and I would wake up and everything would be fine. From a distance I could hear the ambulance. In my heart I felt it was too late. I lost him.

Then the doctor told me that his stab wounds were minor and he was going to be all right.

"Juan, what would I have done if I lost you? What about Alegria?"

His eyes filled up with tired tears that expressed so many words to me. He didn't say a word. He didn't have to. A few days after the incident, Juan and sus homeboys were kicking it at our canton. Juan told me that they were celebrating his second chance de vida. Everyone was kicking back, drinking up and listening to oldies. I was so tired I decided to go to bed.

"Juan ya me voy a dormir."

He grabbed my arm, "No Angel quedase con migo."

I was surprised by his words—but by the look on his face, I could tell he was a little intoxicated.

"No Juan, I'm tired."

He pulled me close and whispered, "Chiquita, I'm sorry."

I looked up at him, "For what?"

He took a deep breath and hesitated to speak.

"Angelica, my little Angel."

He was holding me so tight. I was confused by the way he was acting. I lay on the bed that night wondering why he was saying

ILLUSTRATION BY
VICTOR A. SPIDER

sorry. Did he mean it?

I woke up to a horrible feeling in my chest. I found myself lying in a lonely bed. It was four a.m. and Juan wasn't home. I began to panic. Where could he be this time? I stared out the window hoping for an answer. The glittering lights of the city glowed so bright, they looked as if they were dancing.

"Juan, where are you?" I sat in front of the window for five hours.

I watched the sky turn from deep purple to bright orange with still no answer. My eyes felt tired and I could barely open them. I thought they were deceiving me when I saw a police car parked across the street. I stood up to get a better look. I could see the policeman collecting his things from inside the car. I ran to the door and opened it. I was desperate to know what happened. The officer came toward me and asked me if my name was Angela Velazquez, le dije que si. He then asked me if Juan Velazquez lived here. I was in a panic. I could hardly speak.

"Officer, please tell me what happened to Juan."

"I'm afraid I have some bad news. This morning Juan was arrested for first degree murder."

"What? What are you talking about?" I had to hold on to the door because I was so weak from shock.

"Evidently your husband had planned it out, it seems like Juan was trying to get revenge on a rival gang. I understand there was an incident here last week?"

I could not believe what the officer was telling me.

"No, there must be some mistake, Juan would never do a thing like that."

"His fingerprints are all over the weapon. He'll be doing time for quite a while, I'm sorry."

There I was, right back where I started. "This time I swear it will be different," he had said to me, yo no voy a jugar esos juegos. I need to turn my life around and keep living for my hija. I can't cry. Cry for what? Maybe for being a pendeja, for staying with him.

A few weeks later, I was preparing for a little party in celebration of mi hija's first cumpleaños. Una amigita de Alegria me estaba ayudando con los odornos. Her name was Blanca. I remember her so sweet. Her eyes seemed to always light up the room. She loved Alegria, la cuidaba como si fuera su hermanita. Ella me pregunto si podia jugar con Alegria afuera y le dije que si but you have to play where I can see you. Staring out the window watching Alegria play brought me sadness in my heart knowing that Juan was going to be missing out on the most precious moments of his daughter's life. Pues asi es la vida... pesada como una cruz.

As I was cooking, I was overcome by a feeling of great fear. As a matter of fact, I had to stop what I was doing. Through the window I could see Alegria playing pero when I looked up the street... casi me muero. I recognized the car right away! It was the same black Monte Carlo we had problemás with last month! I dropped everything. I felt as if someone stole my breath. I couldn't scream. I was frozen in my own fear. "Dios, mio!" By the time I reached outside, I realized it was too late.

"Alegria!!" Her sweet face turned toward me: "Mami?" Me dijo... and once I heard the first valaso I just closed my eyes and listened to the sounds of death take away my baby. I remember feeling so helpless that I couldn't do anything to save her. I fell to the ground feeling the greatest darkness overcome my spirit. I cried in agony, in pain, and when I looked up, there is no word in this vida to explain the nightmare I was living at that very moment. I swear I'd rather be blind than to see my little baby surrounded in her sweet sangre. Her stomach was all twisted and defaced. This was not happening to me! It was something you would see in a movie, but this was my reality. I crawled to them hoping for some type of miracle to happen. I picked up Alegria from the floor and hugged her so tight.

"Alguien ayudeme por favor!" I turned to Blanca and began to shake in panic. What has happened to her beautiful face?

"Blanca, Blanquita despiertate! Por favor Dios no te las lleves!" I cried in desperatíon.

I held both of them in my arms when Blanca's mother came running out of her house screaming.

"Que paso? Dios mio!" Her face showed horror for whoever's child's life was taken. She didn't recognize the fact that her own child's life was the one to be taken.

"Adónde esta Blanca?"

I stared at the emptiness that slapped her face when she realized it was her hijita que estaba muerta en mis brasos.

On May 10, 1989 my baby was born into this cruel, heartless world, only to be dead exactly one year later because of Juan's own selfishness and immaturity. His games cost our baby's life. It has been four years since this tragedy has happened, but the memory of that day runs through my mind every single second of my life. Today is Alegria's fifth birthday and her memory lives strong inside my heart. Why are the innocent the victims? Sometimes when I look in the mirror and I see my reflectíon, I see a clown face laughing back at me. Am I a fool? Maybe. Juan sends me letters every now and then but I don't read them, I just send them back. Maybe I should have done that a long time ago. Happy birthday hijita... happy birthday...

La Casper
By Casper

The sky was black and the warm summer San Jo winds were blowing. My homegirls and me were walking through the barrio. Suddenly behind us came these other Norteñas. They asked us where we were from and we said proudly, "The north side." We found out that those hinas were from the north side also. It seemed like we were going to get into some shit between us and them. One hina asked who we knew and we named a list of vatos. We found out that she was our homeboy's (who now rests in peace) homegirl. Once we started talking all of us became cool, so we kicked back with them the rest of the night. When we were all about ready to jam back to our pad, one hina gave us her number and said, "If you ever want to kick it call me." I didn't know if we should trust them or not because we met hinas on the streets before that were supposed to be our homegirls that fucked us over. But we put that behind us and called them to kick it. We didn't just kick it once with them but we became hella good homegirls with them. After a period of partying, kicking back and backing each other up, we all trusted each other. They wanted us to get into some click they were in. They said they needed true homegirls like us to be in the click. We gave it a lot of thought and decided to get jumped in. We were all willing to throw down our lives for one another. One night some shit went down with some hinas from another barrio. My homegirl got stabbed and we had to rush her to the hospital. Four days later we went to find those bitches. They needed payback for what they did to my homegirl. We went to the alley where those hinas were kicking it. We rushed them and one hina pulled out her blade so I pulled out mine. It was an accident; she fell on my knife and got stabbed in her side. My homegirls and I left. I looked down and red blood stained my hands. I felt sick to my stomach. I could have taken that hina's life. I didn't know and I didn't wait around to find out. As time went by, I tried to forget that memory.

Over the years, many things happened—partying, fighting, everything that our kind of lifestyle brings. One night when I just turned 18, me, my homegirls and our sanchos went to a get-together that our homeboy was having on the east side. My old man and I were standing out front just kicking it while everyone was inside partying. I looked over and saw a car roll up. There were vatos inside. Then I realized they were from another barrio. At first I didn't realize what hit me, but I had been shot. I was lying on the cement in a puddle of blood. When I looked up everyone was crying and telling me not to die. I guess when they heard the shots they came outside. I was lying in my old man's arms looking up at his face. He was the last thing I saw before I faded into darkness.

As I walked through homeboys and homegirls I read the back of the red and black shirts, they said, "In memory of Casper." When I finally got up to the casket, I looked down at my pale face with the thick red pano covering my forehead. I realized that my familia, my old man, partying, everything was gone. I was gone.

I sit back up here, thinking back to the beginning when I was 14, a li'l chola just starting out, thinking if things would have been different. Who would have known that the hina I stabbed lost her life and four years later I would lose mine to her brother's bullet. But it's too late. I guess that's life in the barrio.

Lil' Spanky

Lil' Spanky ended up in the pinta at the age of 18. He was involved in a small insignificant battle on the yarda. The huras pulled out their cuetes and put all the homeboys on check. Now Lil' Spanky was in the hoyo and within a few weeks he was transferred to another pinta. He was full of rage and pumped up because in that little insignificant battle, he got down like a real warrior without any weapons.

He came up strolling hard, as if he had just earned the badge of courage. Right next door was an older pinto who looked at him and shook his head. Lil' Spanky got mad but didn't say anything. After a few weeks, Spanky got his personal property and fixed up his canton. He hanged a picture of La Virgen and his mom. The older pinto noticed the picture and said to Spanky, "I don't know what's up with that ruca going out with lil' punks like you." Than Lil' Spanky stood up from his bed and said, "Fuck you puto!" He grabbed his toothpaste and threw it at him. (Lil' Spanky was on the lockdown due to some stupid incident.) When the older pinto came back from his jale, Lil' Spanky start telling him all kinds of shit and the older pinto always replied by saying, "You are just a fucking Lil' Moscoso that can't wipe your own ass." Those remarks got Lil' Spanky fired up. One day, Lil' Spanky needed a stamp and he said to the old pinto, "Hey you old fart, I tell you what, if you give me a stamp, I'll let bygones be bygones. I need it so I could send a kite to my jefita. Her birthday is coming up and I want to let her know that I have her picture with me right next to La Virgen." Then the old pinto said, "What? That's a picture of your mom?"

"Simon!" said Lil' Spanky.

Then the pinto said, "OK kid, here's a stamp."

Then Lil' Spanky tripped out because he gave it up just like that.

A couple of days would pass by and the older pinto hadn't said a word. Lil' Spanky was kinda worried and started badmouthing the viejo. Then one day the old pinto came out of his shell, went to Lil' Spanky's cell and said, "Ese, the lady's picture you have hanging on the wall, her name is Maria." Then Lil' Spanky tripped out and asked, "How do you know?" The old pinto replied, "I'm your father, Spanky."

El Parque
By Just Another Pinto

Kicking back on my prison bunk, you know, legs crossed, hands behind my head, just looking up past the ceiling into nothingness. If you really concentrate you can release your soul from this concrete womb and soar off to the future or back to the past. It takes practice to be real good at it, but if your life was such that you did more dreaming than doing, well, you know, it comes easier.

During these times, when I release my soul, I usually end up in the past where I have fond memories. I don't choose the future much because I have this thing about wishing for things out of a fantasy; they just don't happen. I prefer the past because I have already done it so at least it's something true and real. I think of the parque where it all began and I would revisit as many times as I could.

I was new to the hood and already I was being checked out, which put me on my toes for what I knew would come. One day as I passed the parque, about 20 pachucos surrounded me. They knew I just moved in but still asked where I was from. Not that they cared but rather more or less to see if I gave any signs of fear or intimidation. I was invited to the parque and allowed to hang around for a while. One week later, on another invitation to the parque, I was "jumped in" to the hood. I recall that day vividly and I swear I could still feel the patadas I received that day. I recall wondering, "If I am one of the boys now, why am I getting the shit kicked out of me?" It was later explained that the "initiation" was to test my huevos. I thought to myself, "Shit, I could have just told them I had huevos had they asked." But it was customary at the parque. Once I understood the reason for it, as many Chicanas and Chicanos do, anyone can say they have their huevos, but more is required with the Raza. After all, what do you expect? We aren't politicians.

At the parque, I could find homies at any time of the day or night, and each time I'd make a showing I was greeted with open arms as if they hadn't seen me for weeks, yet I was only gone for a day. The parque was a place to go where a teacher wouldn't dare slap me upside the head with a ruler or where I didn't have to make my bed or take out the trash. It was a place where even though I was a part of a group, I was still an individual and expected to stand on my own two feet. But if I fell down, they would encourage me to stand up. To a Chicano or Chicana, that is a big deal.

I remember one day at the parque, we were gathered to war. We had two weeks' notice and everyone had to come down to avenge a wrong done to a few of the homies. There were at least 80 of us, and even the girls were ready to go. The homies wore their khakis, tramados and Sir Guy shirts. Most wore stingy brim hats pulled low over their ears, leather gloves, long trench coats and French toe shoes. The homegirls wore their hair teased high; they looked vicious but fine in their Angel blouses, gray khakis with metal chain belts and white sandals. There were so many people at the parque that it was hard to organize the raids we would run that day. Eventually one of the homies put Juicy Lucy on his shoulders and picked her up for all to see. That got everyone's attention, and we were ready. The plan was to enter the rival's parque from all sides so that none would escape the pleito they started.

When we got to their parque, they saw us and grouped together. Not one vato ran, which we respected, but maybe they should have, because we swarmed on them like flies on a sugar cube. There were rucas there so our homegirls got some action. Back at our parque, we were celebrating the retaliation except for some of the homies who had to stand watch for the placa. It was a night to remember, especially for me because it was my first stabbing. I was drunk with glory and then drunk with wine. Later that night at the parque, I didn't see or hear the placa coming, and before I knew it I was hit on the head with a billy club and cuffed up. All I could hear was, "I told you to drop the knife, punk." I was so drunk, I was still holding the knife with dried blood on it.

That was the last time I saw the parque, because I was arrested for murdering some kid that night. The parque that let me be myself and was my sanctuary was no more, because I killed some kid I never saw before. Now all I have are my dreams and a void in my life that can't ever be replaced or made up. It's lost forever and I have not existed since.

They tell me the city voted to build a freeway right through the middle of the parque. They said it was planned that way to break up "those trouble makers" that hung out in the parque. They were talking about me. I don't want to go to any parques when I get out, maybe my blood will end up on some kid's knife. I'll remember the parque, and I'll go there again, but just in my dreams, and just up until we went on the raid. Otherwise I'll wake up in a cold sweat again and again and again. So long parque! Al rato!

Ralphie Doesn't Live Here Anymore
By Arturo Carrillo

It's 1994 and yet it seems like only yesterday, 1979, and I'm cruising in my '61 Impala. Firme day. I think I'll drive over to Ralphie's house and pick him up, go have some pistos and maybe we can hustle up some feria and score some carga.

Cruising down Central Avenue, I pass by a homie's house and see J.B., Bogart, Oso and Mr. Shark kicking back, having a pisto. I call out, "Quiuvo homies" as I drive by. Five minutes later I get to Ralphie's canton and park my ranfla. I see him sitting down on the chair kicking back.

"Quiuvo carnal," I say. By the look on his face I can tell he's malillas.

"Orale homey, como estas?" he asks.

"I'm doing all right carnal, hanging in there, sabes?" I say.

"Ese Tudy, I heard there's some good carga here in town. The vato said I could test it for him, pero no tengo raite. You think you can take me down to the vato's house, carnal?"

"Simon, I'll take you down there." I could tell that Ralphie was almost desperate. "Vamos carnal," I said. We got in my ranfla and headed out.

I started shooting dope when I was 15 years old because I was awitado with my ruca. I started snorting first and one day, when I was going through changes, Ralphie told me to shoot the carga. And since I didn't know how, he volunteered to shoot me up. After that first time, I fell in love. I loved carga more than my ruca and even more than myself. It seemed to make me feel like I was on top of the world and like I had no problems. The trouble was, I had to stay loaded to feel that way. And then there was the malillas...

We drove down Fairview Road to Jose's house. Jose was a Mexicano who sold carga but didn't use. He was in it for the feria, and whenever he got some new carga he would ask one of us to test it for him. We parked and Jose came out. He invited us into his house. On the table was a plate full of carga, a scale and balloons to bag it. My stomach started turning as I saw the carga and wanted a fix. Ralphie beat me to the punch as he called "First!" He tore off part of a matchbook to use as a scoop and dipped into the carga. He dropped the carga into a spoon, picked up 60cc of water, squirted it onto the spoon and lit some matches to cook it. The smell of the sulfur from the match made me sick to my stomach and I almost started throwing up in anticipation of a good fix. Ralphie dropped a cotton ball made out of a cigarette filter and started drawing up the carga, which was now a brown liquid. His used his bandana to tie off, hit himself, registered blood in the syringe and shot up. After he shot up, he managed to release the bandana from his arm and all I remember him saying was, "Hum, good carga," as he went out.

Ralphie died that day of an overdose. Since then Little Stevie, Big Al, Oscar "With the Reds," Dracula, Jimmy and other carnales from the neighborhood have all overdosed and died. The rest of us are either in the joint or on parole. Pisto, carga, yesca, coca, PCP— it's all the same. Black, white and brown, it destroys us all. Yet we Chicanos are on the low end of the economic and social totem pole. We are already struggling, carnales y carnalas, and then we throw drugs and alcohol into the game and become even more oppressed as a people. We need to learn to say "no" to these destructive vices and "yes" to education, sports and a positive mindset. We may have lost a generation already but the future is ours. We need to reach our young people before it's too late.

Young people use us, use me as an example of what not to do so you won't end up dead or in the pinta. I plead with you, open your eyes to the dangers of drug and alcohol use. The result is death or pinta for the rest of your life. Don't believe for a moment that you're immune, it just hasn't happened to you… yet. Give yourself a chance and by doing so, you'll be giving us a chance as a proud Raza to live on and have someone we can look to and proudly say, "I want to be like him or her," a true role model of a proud people; Chicano power at its best.

May the lord bless you all.

CHANGING EVIL WAYS

From a Solid Gang Member to a Grassroots Community Organizer and a Born-Again Christíano: Mike Garcia

Mike Garcia de Bienestar Human Services y Rey de *Mi Vida Loca*

My parents were proud Mexicanos who chose the pachuco lifestyle, and since birth my lifestyle had already been chosen to me. My jefe was very proud of his Mexican heritage and was a strong male role model. I recall many times he enforced the idea that boys don't cry. He had expectatíons of me and my fist-fighting abilities because I was his son and he had been a boxer as a teenager. Unfortunately my jefe passed away when I was five years old. My jefa was also strong and proud. She raised me and my siblings without any government help. She labored in factory jobs and due to financial hardships we moved around different parts of East Los Angeles. We eventually ended up sharing a home with my abuelita and tíos in the Aliso housing projects.

My tíos became my influences and role models. They all belonged to a gang referred to as Cuatro Flats. They were my idols and instilled the idea that I was not to tell anyone about the things I saw or heard and advised me as to what I should or should not do in order not to be a "sissy." I was taught to give 100% so when I became a fully pledged gang member at age 13, I was sent to the "front lines." From that time on, everyone would refer me as Cubano from Primera Flats. I went out looking for pleitos in schools, at parties, on the calles and later in juvenile hall. Later I engaged in stabbings, shootings, "courting" other guys into the gang and violating rival

gang territory. I did whatever I had to do for the barrio. By 15 I was dealing drugs, weed, pills (reds) and eventually heroin. At age 16 I started using it.

As a homie I got shot four times. One day, in front of a school, a rival gang member walked up and shot me and my homeboy. My homeboy got shot in the brain. Later, in my early 20s, my best friend and I were involved in a gang fight, in which he got stabbed in the heart. I tried to stop the bleeding but I couldn't. I knew then that he was slowly dying in my arms. Later that day, my best friend died in the hospital. To society, his death meant just another fatality statistic from gang violence, but to me it meant a lot. He was my best friend.

To top things off, I used and abused heroin and became seriously ill from this addictive drug. I eventually got a disease in which my own body began to suffer. The disease is called phlebitis. My blood became clogged up and became paralyzed. For months I had to relearn to walk. I had this disease for a year, in which I became my own victim.

REY DE *MI VIDA LOCA* MAGAZINE Y ROBERTO "SPIDER" DE SAN FRAN

It was no surprise due to my lifestyle that I had been in and out of county camps, youth authorities and state prisons. Living in these institutions held no hope for rehabilitation. In fact, many times it represented another place where the struggle for power existed. I found myself involved in the race riots between Mexicans and blacks. As a result, I spent time in solitary confinement. The times at the institution were preoccupied with the idea of surviving from day to day. I remember going to the dentist in prison to get a tooth filled; instead the dentist broke my jaw.

The cycle of gang violence continues within one's own family. For example, there were times when my own brother and I did crimes together. Once while we were robbing a drug dealer, a shooting took place and my brother was shot twice. He survived only to die from complications from methadone use. Presently in my family, I have three stepsons and three nephews who have all been shot. Unfortunately, one did die.

After my release in 1996, my daughter, who was only a few months old, was at risk of being put into a foster home because there were traces of a controlled substance in her bloodstream. I decided to take her and hide her for three months. I did this to protect her from falling into a life of institutions in which she would become part of a system that many times mistreats innocent victims. Her jefita was able to hide her for three months.

The insight from being a former gang member and knowing the consequences of that affiliation are by no means something to be proud of. However, that is what makes family and non-family gang members seek to talk and be comprehended. It is through the many challenges that I have learned my lessons. It is not to say that there have been no positive moments, the few that I have come to appreciate are the ones that made me desire a change in my life for the better.

A positive thing that happened while I was in prison is that I got involved with the Chicano movement. When I was released,

I continued being an activist. I participated in demonstration and protest for the Chicano movement. I became a Brown Beret and a member of Mayo. What really changed my life around is that at age 40 I became a born-again Christian. I spent three years living in a church where I slept on the floor. I became the home director and a Bible studies teacher for Victory Outreach Church. Also, in 1996 I returned to my old neighborhood. Now every Friday I go to pray with different gang members. I give presentations in continuation schools, public schools and juvenile hall.

Now I'm currently working at Bienestar Human Services. I have the opportunity to be the lead outreach counselor specialist in my department. I had the flexibility to implement specific outreach techniques into the program, which has made our team of outreach workers very distinguished throughout the community. One of the implementations we use as a risk reduction strategy is handball tournaments. These tournaments are put together by our team and offered to rival gang members as a way to decrease violence. Gang members are awarded trophies for their efforts, which are financed by our agency as well. I have also had the opportunity to present on conflict resolution and gang prevention. I also continue my work in providing one-on-one counseling with these high-risk populations and would not be able to do so without the support I continue to receive from my employer, Bienestar Human Services. In addition, I give presentations that focus on STDs and HIV prevention to different gangs in an effort to promote self-preservation. Many times this also included assisting with the organization of a neutral site where gang members can get tested for communicable diseases.

I enjoy doing this for the youth, mothers and the community. I feel that in helping others I have healed myself. In this effort, I hope to end the cycle of gang violence that was so much a part of my life in the past. My goal is to leave a positive impact on society, even if it is one at a time.

Mr. Garcia has worked and continues working with other grass roots organizations in an effort to help others. For example, he supported the causa to bring justicia to Arturo "Smokey" Jimenez, who was murdered by Jason Mann of the East L.A. Sheriff's Department, assisted in helping the homeless count in Boyle Heights for the Census, assisted at Dolores Mission Church to help feed the paisanos que no tienen papeles and the list goes on and on.

Interview: Ex-Gang Member Roberto "Spider" Rey de *Mi Vida Loca* y Roberto "Spider" de San Fran

MVL: What is your background?
Spider: I am an ironworker, have my GED, and am an ex-boxer and ex-gang member.

MVL: What nationality are you?
Spider: Costa Rican.

MVL: Why did you join a gang?
Spider: We started Ghost Town 30 St. to party and pick up ladies, but it turned out different.

MVL: Are you still in it?
Spider: No, we still get together to party, talk about the old days and listen to oldies.

MVL: What do you think of today's Raza youngsters?
Spider: They have a lot to learn. Back then we got together to party down and took care of business when it came down to it. We didn't have drive-bys; we got out of the cars and went off straight chingasos. Now, they join gangas because they think it's cool and don't know the meaning of partying and kicking back.

MVL: What mistakes have you made in the past which you have learned from and would like to share with the Raza youngsters?
Spider: Being in a clicka will get you in jail soon or later. I wanted to be a Marine but my record kept me from it. I got kicked out of school for hanging around with the homeboys, which kept me from getting a diploma, but later I got my GED.

MVL: What gangs did you fight?
Spider: Besides Raza rivals, we fought flips, mayates, white boys— whoever started shit.

MVL: What message do you have for young Raza?
Spider: Instead of fighting each other, unite! Fight for what we need, like better jobs and a better environment in our barrios.

MIKE GARCIA
DE BIENESTAR
HUMAN SERVICES
AND REYNALDO
DE *MI VIDA LOCA*
MAGAZINE

Been There, Done That, Did It!
Vatos de los Avenues

MVL: Ora! So now that you vatos have changed your evil ways, what advice can you give to our young "Brown-n-Proud" locos y locas out there in Califaztlan?

Ben (Chuco): It's been 13 or 14 years since I haven't been into any activities. I grew up as Chuco from the Avenues, went to juvie, YA and the pinta. Due to gang violence, I lost my little carnal Tiny. I felt gacho cause my carnalito got shot during a drive-by. I had goals for my carnales 'cause we have a family business and my goals were to help the jefito expand the business. Now I lost my jefito and inherited the business. My jefe is proud that I took over the family business and I'm helping my jefito's dream come true.

MVL: What advice do you have for our young "Brown-n-Proud" locos/as?

Ben: To the chavalos and homegirls, I advise you to take life a little more seriously. Get your education and go for your goals for a better life.

Vince (Spooky): I been through the same; been in trouble all my life, juvie and then straight to the joint. This shit gets old and I'm not getting any younger. I have three chavalos—a 16-year-old, 10-year-old and an eight-year-old. If I go back to prison, what good would that do my chavalos? So right now I work with Chuco and in return I'm helping my chavalos.

My advice for young Raza is that you are going around killing yourselves off and that's not the answer. La Raza is not going anywhere by killing each other. Get your education so you can make something out of your life.

Stretch: As for me, I grew up uncontrollable so I got awarded to the courts. From 12 to 16 years old I was in a boys' home. My mom and dad used to come and see me and I would cuss at them and tell them to leave! I had a lot of hatred inside of me. When I was 14 years old they killed my mother and they never let me go to the funeral. Up to this date, I always wished I could have told her that I loved her. When I got out at 16 years old, I was looking for love and that's when I bumped into my homeboys. I became a homeboy from Los Avenues in Los Angeles. Being a homeboy was fun for a while, but then you find yourself doing time in the pinta and sometimes your homeboys are not there. I did a lot of prison time, was there three times, and the thing that I noticed is that your worst enemies sometimes become your best friends.

I thought about the people I hurt in my time, and for what? But now I see things a lot differently and it hurts inside to see my brown carnales/as kill each other for a street name. It's been 13 years since I been out of the pinta. I go to different places to talk to our young Raza about gang violence, 'cause if we don't open up our eyes, we will slowly but surely die or end up in prison for the rest of our lives.

SPOOKY Y
STRETCH
DE LOS AVENUES,
LOS ANGELES

Bobby Castillo de American Indian Movement

I am a Chicano-Indio from Fresno. I spent 14 years in the pinta for bank robberies. There I met Leonard Peltier and realized that Chicanos were Indians and that the U.S. government had been waging a war against the Chicano and Indian movement because they feared we might unite.

I spent the last 14 years at Marion Federal Prison, which is considered the most maximum federal security prison. I was placed in a controlled environment where I was given numerous drugs to change my behavior and way of thinking. When I got out I became a counselor, working with youth gangs, and became a full-time political activist. I realized a long time ago that the U.S. government is responsible for the drugs and violence that occurs in our barrios. They realize that Raza are the majority in the Western hemisphere, and if we are to unite, they could never stop us from gaining our land and freedom.

We are all Indian people, whether we are full-blooded or mestizos. We still have Indian blood in our veins. I feel that as Raza we have to direct our pride against the real enemy (the system). We claim that we are down for the barrio and kill each other to protect it, but in reality it's not even our turf. The stores get our money and take it to other neighborhoods so we don't own it. We became tenants in our own land! And invaders became the landlords!

I dream of a day when La Raza unites in the struggle to regain the land. It makes me happy to see our young children becoming culturally aware, joining different Aztec dances and doing indigenous activities. We have to reach out to the chavalitos to get them into that direction instead of the direction of senseless drive-by shootings or taking the lives of their very own race. Our young peo-

ple have learned to emulate prison life and pintos—which means only one thing, you prepare yourself to go to prison. I have never in my life known better warriors than Raza. I understand the feuds and warfare that exist today, and it is going to take the leaders of those clickas or groups to save our youth.

STRETCH, CHURO Y SPOOKY DE LOS AVENUES, LOS ANGELES

MVL: What do you think of the sur/norte conflict?
Bobby: It has gone through many changes over the years and is one of the most senseless things that I can think of. I say senseless because I seen good brothers on both sides, and north-south has to unite, to become educators—not white man's education, but our own! Then the U.S. government and its citizens will be hiding under their beds. People have to remember that our revolutionary leaders were political before going to prison, and some woke up in prison and agreed that their problem was the gringo invader. The U.S. today has a very big problem, and it is us! This is why they are passing laws to make war zones at the borders. They want to use our military troops because the U.S. government fears what will happen if Raza were to unite!

MVL: While in the pinta, how many pleitos were started by the guards so Raza could kill each other?
Bobby: The majority of the pleitos were started by guards. For example, they would set up Raza by putting someone from the north up to a tier of mainly southerners. The guards know that that is like feeding Christians to the lions. Most of the time Raza were too proud to check in or go into protective custody, so they stay to suffer the consequences.
MVL: What is the future of a youngster if he becomes a member of a prison clicka?

Bobby: There is no future! His future is to live in an isolation unit in the pinta.

MVL: In the past, Raza used to get along. Describe how.

Bobby: We used to be able to walk the streets and go to another barrio; instead of getting "dog" the vatos used to say "orale." That was back in the '60s. The white man realized the danger of our unity. Leaders of the Chicano movement were either murdered or put in prison. Our barrios were infested with drugs and weapons and now we are in this mess. The white man probably goes to sleep with a smile on his face every night because the natives are fighting amongst themselves instead of against them.

MVL: Ese, how do you want to conclude the interview?

Bobby: In conclusion, we see white people talking about how they are tired of their government and tired of racism toward people of color, but they only mean black people. For example, if Rodney King would have been Raza it would never have made the six o'clock news!

In the L.A. riots, more Raza were sent to jail, more Raza businesses were burned and more Raza died than any other race! But the media only portrays it as black injustice and Korean injustice. It's time that the media starts portraying the truth.

Why is Raza the majority in Pelican Bay? There are more Raza in segregation units and isolation units all over the southwest, but the media only makes it a black and white issue, and never shows the brown side of injustice.

MVL: Simon! Our suffering and loss is never significant to them. It's time to let non-Raza know that we are here! The sleeping giant has awakened! Y que!

Bobby: Prison is not a good life. But the white man does not want us to have a good life anyways. Before joining a gang, think about joining a revolution. Instead of fighting Raza you should be uniting Raza.

La tierra es nosotros! When we take the land back, then we will be able to end our problems. You can't have freedom without land! I guess they call the U.S. a free country because they never paid us anything for it. It's time to come together and serve eviction notices! Raza youngsters have the right to be proud, but let's learn to be proud together instead of divided.

MVL: "La union hace la fuerza."

14.

PINTO'S CORNER

Messages From Within the Walls
By a Chicano Pinto

I woke up one morning to the smell of the jefitas cooking. There was a mixture of huevos rancheros, refried beans, chorizo, hot handmade tortillas with butter and leche. I got up, walked past my little brother carefully so as not to step on him as he slumbered on the crowded floor next to yet another brother and primo. I went to the escusado, turned the water on and gazed into the image in the mirror. I was compelled to ask, "Who am I?" I did not have a ready answer and this fact scared me, I mean, like, doesn't everybody know who they are? After I washed my face, brushed my teeth and slicked back my hair with Tres Flores, I went into the cosina, gave the jefita a genuine hug and beso and asked her, "Ama, who am I, who am I really?"

My jefita looked at me with pride in her deep brown eyes and says, "Mijo, I have waited to hear you ask that question for 15 years and now that you have, I am finally assured that mijo has grown into awareness. It saddens me that you can't learn who you are in school, as many books of history that there are you would expect to have one about the Raza. That part should tell you something all by itself, for if you are left out of the history books in a country where you live, have grown up in and fought for, then you must surely learn something from it. Mijo, your righteous beginning goes way back to the Tolteca who ruled this part of what's known as North and South America. From their history you can find your beginning. But that is not your only make-up, for in your veins runs yet another strain of noble blood, that of the Spanish conquistador. Mixed together you are both, and a part of each. Had the conquistadores not invaded this world then you would have been one of the proud and fierce tribes who lived here like the Azteca, Maya, Inca and many others. Down through the years you had your land taken away, your history almost destroyed and then a barrier put between you and your people. The gavacho calls it a border. You grew up looking at black and white faces where your language has been butchered, and you were made to take a step back from the rest. Even blacks were preferred to you. The person you are today depends on how well you preserve who you are. Listen mijo, just because you must máster the English language, in order to get by in this country, doesn't mean you have to turn your back on the true tongue of your people. Just because you live around whites and blacks does not mean you must imitate or copy them, because you have nothing to be ashamed of. Your blood of the Tolteca and conquistador is something other races wished they had. You grew up in cities apart from your homeland and you adopted and changed some. Today you are Chicano!"

Raza, who are you if you think white and act black? The answer is that you have given up your identity and are a lost being. You can't even look your people in the eye and see yourself, because you are slowly and voluntarily draining your heart of this noble blood all on your own when you abandon your Chicano ways for those of any other race! The gavacho doesn't have to kill us off by putting us against each other in the streets, prisons or even across borders. Each time a young Chicanita or Chicanito turns up on a rap song and says, "Wazz-up" with his hands folded across his chest, he is killing off his own identity. Preserve your "Chicanismo" Raza, hold your head high with pride that you don't live in someone's shadow.

The Black and White Syndrome
By Just Another Pinto

Have you noticed lately how TV seems to portray only black and white people in the movies and commercials? From billboards by the highway to advertisements on the radio and newspapers, there seems to be a "mindset" that the only people in the good ole' U.S. are either black or white, and nothing between.

What about the Raza? Where do we fit in? Or do we? We know we are here and we know we exist but who else knows? By keeping Raza off the TV are we being told that we are not acknowledged? Are we purposely being left out of the spotlight so that we gain no notoriety?

Turn the channel on your TV from *General Hospital* to the news. You find a white face interviewing a black one on how he is homeless or discriminated against but nothing reflecting any of the injustices our Raza faces every day. Why is this? Are we not also of some significance?

By excluding Raza from TV and movies and the media, are we being told that the white man prefers the company of the blacks over us? Are we not as worthy of recognition as the blacks? Or are the blacks the lesser of two evils, you know, like as if the white man sat down and decided that he will have to lay down with either the blacks or the Chicanos for appearance's sake, and then chose the blacks over us?

Does this question make you think about yourself and your status in this country? I hope so, because it's pretty obvious that we are being left behind. Consider all the black-only colleges in the country—whites helped build them. How many Chicano colleges do you know of? Whites have even gone so far as to allow black men to jump in bed with white women on their soap operas and allowed mixed couples in their sitcoms. But how many Chicanos do you see swapping spit with pretty white girls on TV? Why is this? Are we the new mayates of the U.S.?

The only time Raza makes a showing on TV is when they're involved in crime. Where's our Rodney King? Don't Chicanos get their heads caved in by the placa? Or is it that placa putting Raza in the hospital for jaywalking doesn't merit the top story on the six o'clock news?

The sad part about all this is that Chicanos and Chicanas are too busy stabbing each other in the back to notice what is happening to us. While we allow ourselves to be dismissed by the gavacho, we slowly disappear as a race, with no voice in what happens to us.

All you have to do in order to be left out altogether is to continue to be just a little voice, on a little street corner, in your little neighborhood, to your little homies—because while you're holding down the hood (that the gavacho owns), the rest of the world is passing you by and sweeping you under the rug. A street gang has no future, little brothers and sisters. You don't go anywhere, you don't see nothing and you can't get anywhere gangbanging. You can't use your hood as reference when applying for a jale, the jale you need to feed your chavalos and the jale you need to have respectability. The only future you have as a gangbanger is a stretch in the pinta with the rest of the gente that couldn't make it in the real world.

Right now as you read this article, there's another story being told on TV about another chino or another Russian immigrant who came to America with $20 in his pocket and is now a millionaire! Most of those people didn't even know how to speak English, and yet they found ways to give their families everything they need in this life. How many gangbangers can send their children to college? How many can afford to take their rucas off of the welfare lines? How many vatos locos even hang in school long enough to graduate?

It's time to open your eyes and look and see what is happening to our people, how the gavacho acts like we don't exist and how the mayate is passing us up as well as every other non-Latino race.

I see a day when a "vato loco" means a Chicano with street sense who unites all his homies in a collective, makes sure they are organized and educated on how to run and expand a business and who turns around and pulls in another "loco" to give him the game on prosperity. I see a day when our beautiful brown carnalitas not only finish school and go to college but who also demand that if a vato wants to be with her then he has to accomplish what she has. I see a Chicana who wants more out of life than to depend on welfare instead of her vato taking care of business like a man.

I see these days in the future because I know we as a people have more heart and courage than any race on the face of the Earth, and we prove it every day of our lives. But we have to apply that same corazon we have toward things that bring us up instead of down. If you can show the same heart you show when you stand up along 10 vatos defending your hood, to finishing school and going to college, then there's no mistaking that the vato loco will be on top.

Imagine for a moment, a vato loco from the hood becoming an attorney, a doctor, senator or businessman! Yet the vato is the same person you call homie. The only difference is that as a businessman the homeboy can turn around and pick another homie up off the street and teach him the way to have things. Just because you make the move to get ahead in life so that you won't be left behind doesn't mean you have to give up being who and what you are. Rather, it means you'll be in a better position to really help your gente, familia and your future. Reynaldo, the editor of *MVL*, is a vato loco that refuses to be put in the back seat of life and is doing something about it. My respect goes out to him especially because he is trying to take all of you with him and at the same time has not lost his identity. He walks, talks and feels as all of us, except his heart is with us instead of against us. He is trying to wake us up to the harsh realities that are common to each of us but which we refuse to acknowledge. He asks nothing of us except that we save ourselves from destroying each other. The least we can do is to think about how much longer we will allow the gavacho to pass us up.

Get with the program, gente, before we get pushed into the ocean.

No-Win Situation
By Sundown

It's a stacked deck and a no-win situation... they're holding all the cards. But you want to be a tuff guy; you're not afraid to die. Well let me tell you, brothers, the dying part is easy; it's the living that's hard.

You've got three strikes against you from the day you're born. And there's a lot more to life than cruising and blowing your horn. You had better pay attention to all the laws they are passing down, 'cause you'll find yourself before them and they'll treat you like a clown. You'll say, "You can't do that!" And they'll say, "Yes we can, and we just did!"

Welcome to the real world; no one's gonna miss you. You're just another stupid kid. You'll be caught up in the human livestock game, filling prisons so they can live. They'll send their kids to college and take vacations on all the years and tears, misery and blood that you can give.

When you think that your time is done, let me tell you, son, you've only just begun. They'll recycle you like aluminum and give you twice as much time for the time you've already done. So if you wanna play, be ready to pay... with all the best years of your life.

You can forget all about the drive-by warfare, because in here, it's face-to-face... close up and in person... toe-to-toe with a knife. There ain't no more tough guys, just human cattle in a state prison,

bringing the másters their paychecks amounting to billions every year. And once you're caught up in their system, they'll never let you go, 'cause you're a money-making steer. If you want something to be angry about, then be angry about the fact that from the day you were born you were being groomed for being here.

'Cause it's all the money, sonny, and poor people have a part to play too, even if it's just breeding sons and daughters to become human cattle in the concrete prisons built by the contractors and politicians who profit from these human zoos.

You wanna be a tuff guy doing drive-bys? The next time you're in the car thinking you're some gangster movie star, just remember that the gates to hell never close and they've got a place for wanna-be tuff guys like you right here beside me in this human zoo. And if you happen to kill some child or some old lady, oh well, shame on you, 'cause you won't have to find me, believe me, I'll be looking for you, with a very special welcome that's stiff and hard and penetrates the lives of punks like you, you imitatíon tuff guy. 'Cause drive-bys are cowardice, and I told you, "It's a no-win situatíon!!"

Chicano Tragedy
By Darren Garcia

Locked in time are we... The incarcerated Chicano imprisoned in a labyrinth of concrete walls and steel doors trapped in the utter madness that is Pelican Bay State Prison. Known by the tenants as the "End of the World," most traces of humanity have been erased from our now-sordid lives. Even the sun has been extinguished by our keepers, who do not permit us to enter into the equatíon of nature. Rather, we are force-fed a steady diet of mental anguish, solitude and isolation, forbidden to be who we are, the ever-proud descendants of our beloved Aztlan! We are society's faceless and discarded human waste, who could not be trusted with our own dismal fates. Forgotten sons who dare not dream of a world beyond our perimeters governed by our captors, who yearn to find some hidden passage out of this fortress of perpetual time, to take us back to our barrios and the lives we left behind so long ago...

I often wonder if barrios still stand or if they too have perished from the face of the earth like the once-mighty temples and pyramids of Tenochtitlan? Where are the children? The forsaken 60 percent who live only in memory of their father's name, scrawled across some city fence? Like indelible symbols of their former selves. True barrio warriors who carried banners of their calling with heads held high, back ever to the wind, making future attempts to reclaim a piece of tierra stolen from us long long ago...

We ran about the streets like creatures of the night seeking our fame and fortune in an impoverished landscape. That landscape offered us little hope and gave us only the bumps and bruises that our broken and bullet-ridden bodies bore from the countless street wars fought throughout the barrios of Califas. Chicanos chasing down Chicanos as if they were raptors in some primordial hunt for wild game. But a game it was not! Much blood was shed along with all the hopes, dreams and ambitions of a tomorrow they will never see. We were disenfranchised men who saw ourselves as dispensers of life's tragedies. Young men who harbored little regard for a society incapable of embracing us as equals and acknowledging our inherent worth as human beings! In our apocalyptic world, the inner city, a pool of crime and poverty orbiting upon a bloody axis, we were systematically relegated to the bottom of society and painted as the worst of the worst. Dysfunctional, illiterate dregs who could not function on our own, but had to be chained, warehoused and controlled by the state.

We were separated from all that defined our character to be rebellious and our behavior recalcitrant—thus, the Chicano with an unremitting fighting spirit for a better tomorrow was made a prime candidate for Pelican Bay's infamous SHU (Security Housing Unit), a prison environment designed solely to test an individual's threshold for unabated pain and physical abuse. As though we deserve nothing better than a steel-toed boot to the face and body. This is the existence that many of us will never escape. Invisible to society and mute to the world. Half-men who live in the shadow of confinement, pacified and numb. Unable to touch, feel or hold our loved ones. It is obvious to me as I endure this period of incarceration while spitting in the face of social injustice, that 10 or 20 Pelican Bays erected on the morrow will not alter the crime rate one iota! There will always be a need to pour billions of dollars into prison after prison in a feeble attempt to segregate the "Chicano" as an outcast of society. So long as we continue to spawn chavalitos who sadly will never come to know or learn about such proud, great men such as Diego Rivera, Rufino Tamayo, Octavio Paz, Carlos Fuentes and José Vasconcelos. Raza men with vision who sought to enlighten the minds of Chicanos and all Raza alike. They will never know who they truly are, nor where they came from. If this trend of a society's attempt to "whitewash" us continues to exist, the uncertainty of our future Raza, will continue to burn in all of our hearts and minds... forever.

"Carnalitos y Carnalitas"
By Your Carnal Javier

Qvole carnalitos y carnalitas. You have already made your first step in the betterment for our Raza by reading this magazine.

The things I have to say are up to you as to how you're going to take them. But think about what I say, filter it through your mind and then speak your version to the next homie. Because we need to get the word out. We are losing too many of our brown brothers and sisters to these other races.

I'll start out by saying: What are we going to do about our lost brown brothers and sisters? I call them the Lost Raza. The ones que think they're gavachos or mayates. That really makes me mad when I see a fellow brown brother or sister thinking they're better than us because they grew up on the white side. They even

"WHY" BY TOCATL
BY R. GOLDE

sometimes try and make their name sound gava. For example, I knew one that instead of writing her name A.R.C.E. would write R.C. because they said it sounded more American. We can't have that. Then we have estos gueyes that think they're mayates. They wear them X hats and say they're "pimping." Then what happened to our Varrio Turica? Now they want to use ghetto rap. We got to wake up and smell the beans, because these idiots have it smelling like that perm kit mess.

I know it's the Pepsi Generation and everyone wants to get along as that punk mayates said. Well I have to say we can't be listening to mayates, and another thing: If we can't get along with our own, why should we be trying to get along with everyone else?!

OK, here's some fuel for the fire in that brown-skinned heart of yours. When them changos were tearing up their varrio, they were not only disrespecting the gavas stores, they were also in ours. When they were beating the crap out of this little old Mexican vato, they didn't make as much news about it as they did with that gava trucker. They really hurt that vato too. They painted his face and everything! Where's the respect my brothers and sisters? What are we, the race to be stepped on? I remember when we couldn't be disrespected like that. Or is our younger generation getting weak?

For those of you that still find them changos to be all right: How would you take it if you caught your carnalita or prima or niece with one? You know the way they treat their rucas. Think about it!

Now here's some of the ways we can get back at the other Razas.

We have to stop buying food from all the other races' restaurants. That goes for all business establishments. Yeah, we might have to pay a bit more—but hey, that's the way the other races did it. And if you go into a Mexican-owned establishment and another kind of race is working there, walk out. I know there are going to be times when we need to go to one of the bigger stores for certain things, but let's try and not make it a habit. This way we will be making an effort to make life better for our kids, and their kids to come, and the future will be ours!

Your carnal,
Javier

Why
By Tocatl

Why must it be that the same hand which can push or pull us forward is more often the one which holds us back?

Why is the chain which holds us to the barrio and a lifetime of suffering stronger than the one which holds us together?

Why is the desire to be a street gang leader greater than the desire to be an inspiration to the people?

Why does the same goal for advancement call for unification of the barrio but separation of the people?

Why do we separate ourselves from each other in our search for a label "Latino" or "Chicano" while we accept the hand of the gavacho and assist in the plight of the Africano? For both of them call us wetbacks and spics and treat us as inferiors.

Why does the Mexicano come to the U.S. and forsake his gente and homeland for the sake of a barrio?

Why do we complain about the system yet do nothing to change it?

Why?... Ignorance! The only solution to this problem is education. We must unite as a people and learn to take our fight to the oppressor and not to each other. We must learn to take pride in who we are and demand recognition.

With that in mind let me first of all mention that it swelled my heart with pride to see with my own eyes the "vision" being aspired to and articulated by Mi Raza in your magazine.

I compare what I'm seeing to modern-day prophets because what's being talked about is what's gonna happen with or without a 100% contribution by all, because as long as there are those of us within the Raza who are boldly willing and bravely able to spread and uphold the revolution of change happening now in our minds, hearts and spirits, nothing can drag it down! We as Raza would rather die on our feet than live on our knees.

The sour and bitter words of the contra-revolutionary "agent provocateurs" who are either by ignorance or stupidity being manipulated or being straight-up sellouts will in time find their dry rhetoric a choke in the throat, as the empty-handed and stagnated repetition of mistakes, failures and straight-up disastrous, outdated modus operandi again fail.

I say this because we as Raza can never be satisfied with crumbs! Until we as a Raza achieve our maximum place in all levels of the world we exist in culturally, politically, economically and individually, we will not stop striving.

In the immortal words of Che Guevara: "We are not the minority!" However, at this moment we are a voiceless máss, a people who have all-too-often taken their cue from the flawed and selfish minds of those who thirst for the leftovers, while the big time moves farther and farther out of reach—but that will not continue!

That has to stop, especially now, in the '90s, as we face a whole new ballgame of renewed racism and discrimination against our Raza. If you need any proof of this just look around you and notice how many brown faces you see in comparison to any other!

More and more gente are simultaneously recognizing what "three strikes" is really all about and what Pete Wilson is doing with the immigration issue and all this prison construction (especially SHU filled to the brim with La Raza).

As we ponder on what this all means, let us not fail to reflect upon our history from the time gringos introduced the reservations and prison concept to Aztlan. Up until now, it becomes a self-evident truth, more and more clear, that if we don't learn from history we are doomed to repeat it.

But from what I'm starting to see, that is not about to happen, though, because we are not blind (like before) to the ways and means that have in the past been used against us to ignorantly mislead us; all the divide and conquer tactics and the agent provocateurs' slanted propaganda and confused bewilderment.

Too many know what time it is. Too many are too mentally sharp than to be fooled or tricked. Too many have the combined capacity of intelligence, wisdom, imagination and cora to go out like that! And in that collectively we as Raza and as men have the power to achieve greatly as we tap into our vast potential.

Within this we are compelled to approach all we now do toward that end in a business-like way, with common sense and logic. We must utilize only the best in a pluralistic and eclectic way. We must be diverse and flexible enough so that we always have the capability to adjust to the specific situation and our objectives as much as possible.

We have before us the benefit of all the past failures as lessons to learn from. We must break it all down examining each piece and only then rebuild from the bottom up and top down.

As a grass roots effort, each man, woman and child individually can and should contribute to this revolution of the mind, heart and spirit or our Raza because we can no longer afford to automatically look at our own Raza with hate, disrespect and contempt because the pride lives in all of us who are worthy of it—it's about that time.

In that regard I'll end this contodo mi respecto y amor to Mi Linda Raza!

Soy RG, Pelican Bay Mexicano!

Portrait of a Guerrero
By Tocatl

I am an extension of what was:

Mexican blood was spilled so that the sun would light my path. El Grito de Dolores was a declaration of my independence and Emiliano took to arms so that Mi Tierra would be returned to me.

My beliefs and will to fight come from the examples of César Chávez, Corky Gonzales and Jose Angel Gutiérrez.

I am a seeker of the truth.

I've dispelled the myth of Columbus' "Discovery" and regard his voyage as trespassing. I realize that the conquest never was, and I know Cortes as the original cachupin.

I've learned about the treacherous dealings associated with Manifest Destiny, the treaty of Guadalupe Hidalgo and the Gadsden Purchase.

I am shaping my tomorrow.

I oppose the government's attack on mi gente and implore the Raza to stand and voice their dissension as well. I will not accept the "Hispanic" label over my own identity as a Mexicano and I will teach my children, brothers and sisters about our culture so that they will hold our values in their hearts.

I will continue to learn, teach and stand.

15.

TODAY'S STRUGGLE

While in college, I got involved in the struggle of my gente. I remember attending La Raza Organization, a student group at San Francisco State University. During meetings we would discuss problems in our communities and suggest some solutions. For example, during the Watsonville earthquake aid was not given to undocumented workers 'cause mainstream aid givers stated that they were "illegal aliens." So, a few of us from La Raza club made presentations in our classes so people could donate their canned goods, clothing and toys, while most of us donated our things from our families. It was firme, 'cause we rented a huge cargo truck to get all the things to Watsonville. Homie Andres, from Chiques, and I drove the truck to Watsonville. Gente were complaining that the distribution center was taking all the good stuff and giving people the old stuff. So we handed everything right there and then to the gente. Then we hit the fields, and the next weekend we did the same.

Before graduating, a homie named Arturo and I organized a Raza club at Aptos Middle School to teach our young Raza about our history and to encourage them to attend college later in life. Homie Arturo left 'cause he became a policeman with the Oakland Police Department. I tried recruiting other college students to give me a hand, but they were all too busy. I realized that La Raza Organization were just a lot of talk, and no action!

Raza college students were always talking behind each others' backs, which led to the creation of another club called MEChA. Then both clubs just fought against each other. I just stayed away and continued doing my own projects without their help, but I got Latino staff and professors to give me some ideas. The one who stood out the most was Alberto Oliveras, a fellow Nicaraguense from the Mission District. He was my counselor and friend. He was always a guest speaker in my workshops and I always brought groups or individuals to his office so he could give them hope and guidance. Alberto, thanks for all you done for me! Tu eres mi carnal!

But in contrast to my friend and counselor, there were a lot of Chicano staff and Latino professors that, when push came to shove, hid behind their doors like scared mouses! No, I take it back! Even a mouse when cornered against his foe will fight back! But not the so-called leaders at San Francisco State University! Here's a little example, Mr. Apodaca, who had a key position as an administrator at SFSU, had plans to hire another Chicano/Latina for his cabinet after he left—but neither he or the other staff or professors wanted to challenge the president. I told him that if he would have had Alberto on his side, Raza would have been walking proud on campus, but instead he congregated with snakes and cowards. So we decided on talking to Raza students to put pressure on the staff and professors. I personally went and talked to everybody, stating that the president's cabinet had nothing but blacks, Asians, whites, gays and lesbians with no intention of putting one of our own in his cabinet to represent our people. La Raza Organization refused to give me a answer, while MEChA stated that they did not want to step on people's toes. So I wrote the following:

Attention Raza at San Francisco State University!

To: Ligeia Polidora, Dir. Public Affairs
From: Reynaldo Berrios, Publishing Editor
Re: An interview with the president

As I stated over the phone, I graduated from San Francisco State in 1992. These are the questions I want to ask President Corrigan:

1. We, La Raza, are the majority of the state of California, yet we don't have any representation in your cabinet: Why? Please explain.

2. How does the cabinet set up policy concerning who is going to get the key positions?

3. What are the different ethnic backgrounds that make up your cabinet? How many of each?

4. I heard that Ed Apodaca is leaving. Who is going to replace him? Is it going to be a Chicano/Latina person?

5. Do you plan to include Raza in making decisions on important issues?

In conclusion, I have worked with Mr. Apodaca on various occasions, where he has talked to Raza kids and teenagers about the importance of education and having a profession. He has inspired and motivated many of our future generation in striving for education; now that he is leaving, who am I going to present as a great Raza role model?

I sent this letter to the Director of Public Affairs for President Corrigan of San Francisco State University, and she said that the president felt that the questions I asked were unfair and that I needed to rephrase them. Now, I don't know how you gente feel about this but, as for me, I'm taking it as if we don't have the right to ask questions nor have the right to have one of our own gente making key decisions.

HOMIES DE
NORTHSIDE
SANTA RITA

Now, what are the "Brown-n-Proud" at San Francisco State University going to do about this? Or are we just going to sit back and let them walk all over us like they have done in the past? And, are we going to keep on being the quiet little mice that don't want to take back our cheese from the mean bad cat?! Mi Raza! We are not a weak people, and if we don't challenge the system then we are just going to remain at the bottom! I don't want us to remain as the quiet lil' mouse that is scared to come out of its hole. Let's organize and plan a strategy so that we, the "Brown-n-Proud," can have a voice inside the president's cabinet. Remember this y gravenselo en la cabeza... If we don't help our gente and if we don't bust a move, then all them other races will have no respect for us!

So if any of you gente would like to organize and bust a political grape, then contact me.

Aqui para mi Linda Raza,
Soy,
Reynaldo

Wake up sleeping giant!
After the response from the president's office, I went back to the student organization and to the staff and professors and they hid away from me when they saw me coming toward them. And Mr. Apodaca said, "Look for them to stab you in the back later, Reynaldo."

"Yeah, the same way they stabbed Alberto Oliveras in his heart," I responded.

Then Mr. Apodaca stated that whether I like it or not I was a leader and to look for my own people to bring me down. I left disappointed because I couldn't motivate the useless people to congregate in a peaceful matter to protest Raza rights on campus by having one of our own people to represent us in the cabinet. Surely, as Mr. Apodaca predicted, another mayate was elected to the president's cabinet.

While this was going on I had joined a community Latino organization to demand good-paying jobs for the homeboys/girls in the Mission District. All the good jales were given to the blacks, whites, gays and lesbians while we got paid minimum wage. And at the end of the struggle, the piece of shit who organized everything got a big sum of money and took off. The last I heard of him, he was going to the hospital due to heart failures.

Then I joined a group of Latinos that demanded a share of funding for our schools in the Mission. We went to the board on the funding issue and lost, because the school board was made up of blacks, whites, Asians, gays and lesbians and they voted against La Raza. Later we met in court and the school board brought in the NAACP, a black organization, and they said that we were too ignorant to know what we wanted for our gente in the school curriculum and that they represented all minorities. So the pinche mayates and gavachos that were school administrators distributed amongst themselves $28 million in federal and state funding. And their little black and white kids received a better education than our "Brown-n-Proud" chavalitos, 'cause we got nothing!

Before this took place, in Los Angeles non-citizen Latino parents were demanding the right to vote on school elections, but the gavachos and mayates were against it. For example, Kourt Williams, co-chair of the Black Education Commission and Herbert Jones from Alliance of African-American Educators said, "by granting voting rights to non-citizens the voting power of blacks would suffer," and called it "disrespectful to blacks." Could you imagine this from the very same people that bitch and cry about civil rights? As for the gavachos, they simply said, "It's silly and outrageous for illegal aliens to vote in school elections." And, ironically enough, gavachos crossed a whole ocean to get here and claim our ancestral land for their own!

Mi Linda Raza, por favor, analyze what I just wrote, think about our present situation and ask yourself how much longer are we going to let gavachos and mayates get the best of everything? For how long are we gonna let them disrespect us in the political, social, economic and legal arenas? When are we gonna stand up and demand our rights? We are in our own ancestral land, and yet they call us wetbacks and we have to accept it! Pues, as a vato que me vale and as a proud Nicaraguense descended from Nicarao I have put all my energies into motivating, educating, planning and organizing our gente for a better future. It's time for each and every one of you to do the same! Stop the chismes! Stop the backstabbing! Organize! Plan our goals and put them into action! Educate your mind! Read books! Learn the new, and don't forget the past. To individuals, go

forward and bring happiness and prosperity to your loved ones. To Raza organizations, stop kissing ass and help our people! There's too many weak minds out there trying to represent a proud race. We need strong men and women con corazon y con huevos! Con la Bendicion del Creador todo poderoso y la Bendicion de Nuestras Antes pasades "Los Indigenas," go forward and make our race proud!

Here are some struggles *MVL* wrote about...

San Pancho Against 187

It's November 9 and the tío tacos, gavacho foreigners and the white-washed Amerikkkans voted for 187. Pues, La Raza in San Pancho organized to protest against these new tactics to bring our gente down. Raza met in the Mission, marched down to City Hall and back to La Mission. 187 is going to hurt our gente a great deal, and it's going to create a bad stereotype of all of us—but we let it happen, because we saw it coming, and our so-called leaders just sat back or hid behind the door. Let this be a lesson to all you young "Brown-n-Proud"; we need some down Raza that will help us come up!

We are tired of all those old kiss-asses that have brought disgrace to our race. Now, the rich gavachos have pulled these types of tactics in the past. Simon, every time the gavachos mess up the economy, every time there's a lack of jobs, they find a scapegoat to blame it on, so they pick on us! Why? Because we are too busy fighting among ourselves, and those that actually make it into the system or into college become either white-washed or black-washed. But all is not lost as long as there is at least one mujer/vato who is down for La Raza.

We are the majority, but we are not exercising our voting power. Gente, we need to register and vote, or we are going to get eaten alive!

HOMIES DE SAN PANCHO, 19TH ST.

Also, we must organize to bring up our issues and start thinking about our future, but we must leave the white and black influences away from our business! In the process, they will both end up backstabbing us after they finish using us. So, organize for the "Brown-n-Proud," no más.

Now let me run down a little bit of clecha. Under the treaty of Guadalupe Hidalgo, La Raza were promised that their property and civil rights were protected. Simon! Even bilingual education was protected. What happened? Pues, the gavacho wanted more and more. So they manifested hatred toward the "Brown-n-Proud," so the regular gavachos would be against us and feel that our land is theirs. Pero "Amerika" is our land spiritually, morally and historically!

During the 1840s, in Califas some Hispanics went along with the gavachos. They wrote the California State Constitution; it was written both in Spanish and English and it stated that La Raza are able to keep their property, language and culture. Also, that all business and laws would be written both in Spanish and English. But as soon as gold was discovered, the gavachos murdered, robbed and raped our Linda Raza. Then, they made their laws to keep our gente down, uneducated and against each other. History repeats itself over and over again. Now, it is your duty to bring up La Raza. And you must stay in la escuelita and move on to college. The system is there, so let's get into it and turn it around so it can work for us, instead of those European foreigners that crossed the ocean and stuck their dirty hands into our indigenous brains. Nuestra raices son de esta tierra y no se pueden arrancar!

Viva La Raza para siempre! Raza educate, the future is ours!

Riot in Salinas—Santa Rita

MVL: Why was there a riot in your barrio?
Vatos: A cop shot our homeboy Gordo five times in the back.

MVL: Why and how did it happen?
Vatos: On January 11, 1993, Gilbert "Gordo" Gonzalez was at 7-11 waiting for a vato so he could sell his cuete. Gordo was drinking a beer when a cop, Eric Walles, saw him. Since Gordo was 19 years old and drinking in public, he threw the beer can in the garbage when he saw the placa. The placa told Gordo to put his hands on the car. Since Gordo had a cuete with him, he ran and the placa shot him in the back five times while Gordo was running.

MVL: How did the riots spark off?
Vatos: On the day of Gordo's funeral, January 14, 1993, the placas were cruising the barrio constantly. The viejitos, madres, kids and homeboys started throwing bottles at the placa. A couple of the homeboys became snipers, shooting at the placas from the bushes. Also, the homeboys were shooting at the placa when they were coming from the freeway. But the placa didn't return fire; instead they took out their K-9 dogs and were biting a lot of gente. The placa blockaded our barrio so that no one could come in or out; a lot of the homeboys were arrested that day. The next day the papers lied

about how the riot started, and we want to make it clear that the placa murdered our beloved homeboy Gilbert "Gordo" Gonzales.

MVL: What happened to the placa that shot your homeboy?
Vatos: Nothing, he's still working.

MVL: How do you feel about that?
Vatos: That placa should get locked up. If we'd done it we would be looking at 16 to life, but he is free and working. Why do cops get special treatment after killing people?

MVL: Oye Juan, J.R., Santana, Lil' Loco, Lawrence, Gabriel and Michael, you vatos need to contact LULAC, MALDEF and a Raza student organization like MEChA (that's if they are down for La Raza), at Salinas State University and Salinas City College to demand justicia and lock up the placa that killed your beloved Gordo.

Keep trucha, for the placa are going to instigate fights among your barrio and the barrios from east, west and south Salinas. They are going to divide you vatos some more so you can kill each other and forget the real enemy. Trucha N/S Santa Rita and take that pig to jail! Organize the vatos, homegirls, viejitos, kids and parents to bring justicia for your homeboy's death. Hasta la victoria!

San Jose Cinco de Mayo Festival

When *MVL* and camarada Neto de San Fran arrived in San Jo, we ran into a few vatos de Roosevelt Parque, who were checking out the firme ladies and ranflas. On our way to the festival, we got mooned by a nalgota de Tracy (qvo!). As *MVL* and homie Neto proceeded into the festival, these firme flicas were taken. There was

BUTT DE TRACY

Raza from all over, and everybody was having a firme tiempo.

In contrast to these, when the rain managed to break up the festival, gente walked toward Santa Clara St., where they were greeted by the cops in full riot gear, on motorcycles and horses. The marranos were pushing our gente like cattle while brandishing their batons; pushing us away from their motorcycles and screaming, "Move away!"

During the fiasco (caused by the cops), my homie and I ran into two Chinese guys and asked, "Hey fellows, what do you think about this fiasco that the cops are creating?" They both answered, "They're just doing their jobs." Then I replied, "How would you guys like it if this was your Chinese New Year's Festival and your people were getting treated in the same manner that my people are getting treated right now?" Then they gave a horrified facial expression, 'cause now it was about their people, so they saw things different.

Every time our gente assembled, which is our Constitutional right, the marranos always came in with their riot gear, brandishing their weapons, pushing around our gente and giving us bullshit tickets. Pues, in San Jo the viejitas, lil' chavalitos and jefitas were getting pushed around like cattle along with the locos y locas. Mi gente, mi Raza, my concern is this: When are we going to get our onda lista so that when injustice befalls our beloved Raza, we will take legal action against the marranos?

One way is to sue them for violating our civil rights. Another way is to register and vote, 'cause all these gavachos voters and politicians are building more jails and prisons, so we could end up there and kill each other (you gente know what I'm talking about!). The gavas are coming up with a lot of initiatives and propositions so that our lives will be harder while they live off of our miscry! So contact

your city hall and ask them for a registration form. You must be 18 years old to vote. One vote can make a difference pero entre todos rifaremos total!

Also, since we don't have a leader of our own, then you the individual loca y loco must hit the libros so we can use knowledge, skills and technology to bring up La Raza and keep the gringo's feet away from our necks.

Aqui Para La Raza, ese Reynaldo de *MVL*

Raza in College

MVL: What is the purpose for marching and protesting at City Hall?
Raza: To bring awareness to the immigrant bashing that's going on. Governor Pete Wilson, Senator Dianne Feinstein and Senator Barbara Boxer are saying that immigrants are draining money from the economy.
MVL: Why are they saying those lies?
Raza: They want to get re-elected, so they are taking advantage of the bad economy and blaming it on the Raza. For the last 500 years, La Raza has been used for cheap labor and as slaves. When the economy is bad, the politicians say that the immigrants are taking jobs, and that is bullshit because no gavacho wants to pick up lettuce or be a dishwasher. So they pick on the Raza, because we are not united.

MVL: What's your viewpoint on Senator Barbara Boxer?
Raza: She said that she was in support of immigrants, but now she wants the National Guard on the borders to keep the Raza from coming back to Aztlan!
Raza: She's like the rest of the politicians, who are cut-throats that compromise their morals.

MVL: How do you feel when the gavacha/cho promise us things in their campaigns; and once they are elected they turn their backs on us and destroy us with their politics?
Raza: I'm not surprised, their laws are made to keep us out of power. I get angry and I know that we can't trust them. We need to help each other, for they are not going to do it. We need to vote in our own people, who are down for La Raza. Our country has history in blaming La Raza, and the system benefits from our misery.

Oakland Raza Uniting Against Racism in the Oakland School System

Raza from Calvin, Oakland High, Roosevelt, Bret Hart, Madison, Fremont and Hawthorne met at Centro to organize so that they could demand their rights from these Oakland schools. The Raza are mad at the schools' administrations and their staff for the following:

They put Raza down by not encouraging us; our high level of expectations are not being met.

HOMIES DE SAN JO

Administrators and staff give us racist remarks by calling us "wetbacks."

They always frisk us to see if we have weapons.

School security are always harassing us and always on us, most of the security are blacks and they favor black students.

They are sexist, always making sexual comments about young Raza women.

The schools are not teaching us about our history and culture, they are blocking our minds as to who we are.

The schools are being racist by celebrating a whole month for black history and only one day for Raza history. That is being racist! This is not only a black and white city, it's also brown and Asian.

The majority of students at Calvin are Raza, yet we don't have enough Raza teachers. We, La Raza, are coming up in Oakland and we need representation. There are a lot of clickas that are present today, and when we kill each other, those in power don't care about us. So, for one day the clickas in Oakland will unite and become one clicka to fight the racist school system. We are going to protest against their injustice. We Raza are tired of the administrators, teachers and staff when they call us wetbacks. This is our land, and we come from a rich, intelligent culture.

Let's unite for a better education!

Voices de Aztlan in San Pancho

MVL: What do you homies think about the flyer that stated Latinos should be removed form the Mission District?

Scorpio: It's fucked up, 'cause we Latinos have been living here for years.
Ghost: Yeah, we've been here first!
Lil' PeeWee: We are the first ones, and we are citizens.

MVL: Simon que yes. We as Latinos and Chicanos were in the United States first! We were here before this land became the United States. Why? Because we have Indian blood running through our veins! La sangre de los Maya, Apaches, Aztecas, Toltecas, etc. We've been here in the "Americas" since the beginning of time. Our race was around way before the white murderers crossed the ocean to kill and steal. And they have the nerve to call our gente wetbacks? When they cross a whole ocean to get here into our land! Years after the white liars and murderers established themselves in our land, they used ancient secrets to keep us hating each other, and kept us ignorant by denying us education. Now we live under their throats, 'cause their system has been established so that we can be kept in jails and among one another. The sad thing is that by the time some of us realize this, we are faced with life sentences and go into another world. So as long as we don't get our act together and claim our human rights, the system will have their feet against our throats. Organize yourselves, and let your voices be heard! Tell the Latino agencies and gang prevention agencies to stop kissing politicians' asses and get them to prepare you for better paying jobs! Stop police from messing with you, and if at all possible, stop the gavachos from buying the Mission District!
Homies: Joining up all the Latinos against the gavachos is impossible, 'cause there's too much hatred and too much bad blood.

MVL: Japan and the U.S. were once enemies, shit, the gavas dropped the bomb on them; now look at them, they are business partners. Deep down in my corazon I know that one day Raza will go against gavachos and take back what they stole from us! Nuestra tierra y nuestras costumbres. Our culture and family should be first priority. Work on that and tell them Latino agencies to go against all these crooked politicians or to resign, 'cause they are not doing nothing for La Raza!

Raza in High School in East Bay

MVL: What are the que pasos here in school?
Raza: We are getting notices from the office saying that we're on probation and will not graduate on time.

MVL: Why?
Raza: They are stereotyping us as troublemakers. When I first got here there were 15 of my homeboys; now there's only three. The school administration judges us wrong.
  – This is a good white school, and they try to get rid of us. They always try to call everything gang-related.
  – The whites, Filipinos and blacks have their own hang-out

in school, and the administration doesn't mess with them. But when we hang together, they break us up.

– The administration don't even talk to us, they just try to kick us out of school. They say "stay in school" to everyone, but when it comes to us, they kick us out.

MVL: What are you ladies and gentlemen going to do about this injustice?
Raza: We are going to talk to *Mi Vida Loca*.

– Try to organize and go to the school board.

MVL: "Try" is not good enough! You will organize and take it to the school board and let your parents in on the action. The gavacho that have power want Raza to be uneducated, for they know that an educated chola/cholo is one of their worst nightmares. So they keep us uneducated by kicking Raza out of schools that will give us a chance in life and place us in schools where we are bound to fail. It's called the "track system." Gavas go to the good schools to become leaders and we go to the schools where we become their peons. Asi que, you can't let them mess with your education, so organize, and *MVL* will back you up on your quest for education and justice.

Voices de Aztlan in Oakley

MVL: 187 went through. What do you think of this ultimate disrespect toward our gente?
Raza: California used to be a part of Mexico, and it's messed up that they are doing this.

– We had a strike in front of the school; our grandparents and parents worked in the fields. We have a right to be here.

– We don't shop at Mervyn's or at the arcade on Third in Brentwood, because they supported 187.

– I don't like 187 because our gente viven a trabajar y bale madre; it's our own fault because we didn't do anything about it. We have a lot of people, but we didn't go to the polls. We need to become citizens and vote! We must start thinking, because we are going backwards. Look at how many Raza we have, and we didn't use that power. This is Chicano country, and yet we let it pass. We are going nowhere. Maybe next time we will wake up. Now let this be a wake-up call.

Voices de Aztlan in Oakland

MVL: Why are you pissed off about the educational system in Oakland?
Ladies: We don't learn shit about our cultura; all they talk about is black history, and they take their time to celebrate their things. But when it comes down to Cinco de Mayo, we don't get support from teachers, but we do it on our own with much pride.

MVL: We are being ignored on TV and in the movies, but when we are portrayed, we are viewed as either "illegals" or "gangbangers."

What do you think of this?

Ladies: No tenemos apollo suficiente para tener buen puesto. So, I think we give up and say "fuck"; since we didn't make it, we'll go back to what we were doing. En las noticias, ellos nunca sacan nada bueno para que ensenen como se supera un latino/a. They always mention the bad things, never the good.

MVL: Esa Goofy, you just gave me a button that says NO 187. Que es NO 187?

Ladies: Pete Wilson esta usando el codigo de muerte, para La Raza, para sacarnos de California y no poder usar los servicios de salud o tener buena educacion. El ocho de Noviembre va aver elecciones para que 187 sea legal. Pero nosotros queremos que La Raza diga NO y vote contra del 187.

MVL: Raza, go vote on November 8 and say Chale to 187! Any last comments?

Ladies: We want to say qvo to all the homeboys: Alex, Cabezon, Casper, Angel, Tony, Che, Pelon y La Nina. From Shorty, Wina, Goofy and Reina.

Raza in College

MVL: We seen 187 coming out, and we just sat back and let it happen. How are you going to educate your fellow students about this act of ultimate disrespect toward La Raza?

Luis: First off, we have to unite together and stand for the causa of education, and march in the streets without violence, because the politicians are watching our steps, and if we come at them with violence, then they will say that we passed 187 because we are animals.

REYNALDO DE *MI VIDA LOCA* MAGAZINE AND HOMIES DE SAN FRAN MISSION

CINCO DE MAYO,
SAN JO

MVL: Check this out: We, La Raza, are the majority of Califas, which means that we have buying power! Gavachos are in this world for only one thing: to make a buck, and they will sell their own mothers for profit. As of this time, different states and some Meso-American countries are boycotting some of the businesses that supported Pete Wilson's campaign against our beloved gente. *MVL* will do its homework and find out which businesses supported that act of treason toward our gente. Remember, we are the majority, and we have buying power. Let's use whatever we have to let our voices be heard without bitching or crying, for we have self-respect and dignity! "America" is the land of the "Brown-n-Proud."

MVL: How many of your homeboys did you try to get to vote?
Luis: Two out of ten voted. The other eight said that their vote didn't count. But for the first time, I got my younger brother to register, and he voted. On November 8, when I came to the house, his face said it all: "I voted with pride for my people."

MVL: Any last comments?
Luis: We have to unite our communities so that we can have a bigger voice. One voice can only go so far.

No Mas 187s on Nuestra Raza
By Raphael Tapia for *Con Safos* magazine

Once again it's on, Raza! California has just passed Proposition 187, a new law that denies health care and education to the "children of undocumented parents." 187 is just that—187 on our Raza. Conservatives, Republicans, racists and closet racists are mobilizing nationwide to deny the human rights of "undocumented" residents.

CINCO DE MAYO,
SAN JO

It is ironic that the descendents of immigrants (Europeans) are pushing this law, as if they were native.

The media continually embraces such racist terminology as "illegal alien." Nuestra gente no somos aliens de outer space, somos indigenas de las Americas. Nosotros vivimos aquí mucho antes de la European invasion de las Americas. Pero, they forget their history all too quickly. It was not until the Mexican-American war of 1846–1848 that the United States stole the land that includes California, Texas, Arizona, Nuevo Mexico, Colorado, Nevada y más. Yet these people have the arrogance to advocate the philosophy of false nativism, also known as the "go back to where you came from" disease. The descendents of immigrants (Europeans) have the gall and the audacity to believe that they have more right to live here than the children of La Tierra. Even some forced immigrants (Africans who were brought here against their will to be sold as slaves) have mimicked the racist voices of their oppressor by saying that Mexicans should go back to Mexico. Fools—this is Mexico.

The theft of this land has yet to be recognized by American schools, and this has led to a misunderstanding of how land has been acquired by this government. Mexicanos are the ancestors of indigenous people who were colonized by the Spanish invaders of 1492. The indigenous ancestors of Mexicanos have crossed today's false border for thousands of years as tribes from the south traded with northern tribes in one of the most extensive trade networks in the hemisphere. The saying is true, "we did not cross the border, the border crossed us." The invasions of 1846–1848 set the U.S. border at the Rio Grande. This is the colonizer border and has never been recognized by indigenous people. Anyone who is not indigenous (European or anyone else) who dares utter ignorant statements like "go back to where you came from" needs to begin to implement their narrow ideology by investing in boats, planes and other modes of transportation so that they can begin going back to Europe.

The real issue is that California is in an economic recession, while politicians like Pete Wilson are blaming "immigrants" for the problems in California, instead of accepting the responsibility of mismanaging taxpayer dollars. Instead of looking at government excess and mismanagement of tax money, 59 percent of California's voters obviously believe that Mexicans and Koreans are stealing their jobs, committing all the crime, etc. Another small detail that is being ignored is that "illegal" residents pay more in taxes than they receive in services. Mexicanos have feared going to the doctor or sending their children to school for years, yet the media paints pictures of Mexicanos crossing the border just to take advantage of welfare at white American taxpayers' expense. Fools, the majority of welfare recipients are white anyway. Usually Mexicanos keep to themselves for fear of deportation; they don't flood the welfare lines or the doctor's offices. In fact, "illegal" residents are medically cared for to the extent that they suffer from ailments that can be cured, but they cannot afford expensive American insurance fees and overblown doctor's bills.

Many teachers and doctors have already vowed to disobey the law

by not cooperating with the INS (Immigration and Naturalization Service—A.K.A. La Migra) or 187 law. One reason is that 187 stipulates that teachers, doctors and other social service providers are held legally responsible for turning in any "suspected" illegals to the INS. This law turns social service providers into junior Migra pigs, many of which have already voiced their opposition to this measure. Yet for others, 187 has been a big green light for racists to actively discriminate against people with brown skin and "funny" accents.

One of the arguments for 187 is that "illegals" are depriving American citizens of health care and education. It is true that not all Americans have access to the best health care available. The rich can buy the best care available while the poor are deprived of the latest technology and best services. But to blame Asians and Mexicanos for this is both untrue and racist.

We should be fighting for socialized medicine. Most industrialized nations have socialized medicine, regardless of the race, nationality or wealth of their citizens. Everybody in the world should have access to the latest medical technology and expertise. For this to happen the rich will have their assets taken and the insurance company pimps will be shut down so that they cannot take money from the poor and give it to the rich. In Sweden, for example, an American tourist who walks in off the street with medical problems will not be turned away from medical attention if it is needed. This is called humanism—you must not turn your back on another in need.

When you do, you are embracing capitalism, dog-eat-dogism and greed. Chale, in the way of nuestros antepasados we must embrace communalism, in which work and wealth are shared. Distribution of wealth: Now that's something to think about. The top three per cent of this nation have more wealth than the bottom 90 percent put together. The rich corporate man is pimping.

REYNALDO DE *MI VIDA
LOCA* MAGAZINE AND
VATOS DE SAN JO,
SAN FRAN Y DECOTO

16.

BECOME YOUR OWN LEADER

Mi gente, we are in deep trouble. For we, as a proud people of Aztlan, have no leaders to lead us to a better economical, political and social status. Pero todavia hay esperanza, 'cause we have ourselves, and so each proud hombrio y mujer has to become a leader. As individuals, we can make changes for the betterment of our beautiful cultura and race! Our strong and proud voices must be heard in the political arena, but we can't bitch and cry about it, we have to do it in our own righteous way! For example, educating our gente about our beautiful past from our perspective! Educating our bronze gente about the laws that hurt us and then encouraging our gente to vote against them. Soon we will become the greatest máss of voters on the face of the earth, and be able to elect our own "Brown-n-Proud" politicians and push them to push laws that will benefit our Linda Raza! In order to get to that point, each one of us must register and vote. It's really simple, just go to your city hall and ask for a voter's registratíon form. Answer the few simple questíons and mail it! Whether you become a Democrat or Republican, it doesn't matter, 'cause they both ignore us and treat us like shit, so we must remind them that we are here too, that we always have been and that we always will be. Porque esta tierra es nuestra! So what are you waiting for? Get off your nalgas and go get that voter's registratíon form! Fill it out and vote, so our children can have a better future.

Now as an illustratíon for a better economical edge for Raza, check these out: I went to Napa to interview the homeboys out there and they mentíoned that a few of them got hooked up with some firme paying jobs by a carnal who was a supervisor. So now, some of them vatos are bringing some feria to help out their familias. Now that's what a macho is supposed to do, take care of his familia. In additíon, we need to invest our feria into our barrios by buying from our own Raza. Just look around. We have all these chains of stores in which they consume our money, but they never put a dime back into our barrios! We are always giving, but we never receive. We need to own our own tiendas or become managers of these chain stores that flood our barrios.

Now, when it comes down to our social condition, what can I say except that we are destroying our own kind! It's gotten so bad that chavalitos and old people are getting killed due to the cowardly acts of drive-by shooters. Our new generation have turned into sneaky chavalas 'cause they no longer uphold the traditional ways of an hombrio, a los puro putasos! Veteranos are not around to give clecha on how we, as a proud gente, should go to battle when everything else fails. I'm proud to say that at an early age I was taught to stand on my own two feet and to honor our machismo ways, 'cause they're our traditional ways. Only you and your foe will get hurt and no one else! A chavalito, a viejita and a madresita have nothing to do with the bullshit that keeps us down! But like I say, our ways have taken a back seat, que gacho! While this goes on our "gang prevention agencies" are too busy kissing ass and making our Raza weak, for they don't address our problem as a Raza problem, which must be treated culturalmente. I mean, it is Raza that is killing Raza, and it should be addressed as a Raza problem. It's our innocent little chavalitos and viejitos that are getting hit in the drive-bys. Now, why don't these so-called community agencies have the guts to tell the other races that Raza are going to start helping their own, so our innocent gente can walk the calles without any fear of our own people shooting at them because some scared puto didn't get off his ranfla to handle their bullshit a cara a cara.

To summarize todo que dicho, mi gente you have a duty to become your own leader, so we can all live a little better among our own people. I hope my palabras will encourage some of you to do something, anything for the betterment of our beautiful cultura and race!

FAMILIA DE SAN JO

Siempre para La Raza,
Ese Reynaldo de *Mi Vida Loca*

During a más firme hot summer afternoon in San Jo, *MVL* asked the following question: Who do you consider a Raza leader today?
Amanda & Yvonne: I wish we had someone to look up to, but unfortunately we don't, so we have to find it in ourselves.
Gente de San Jo: It's up to yourself and the community; everyone has to vote. We don't have a leader, so we must be responsible as individuals.
Reyna de San Jo: Joe Fabila, who works for the church and counsels people in jail.
Ladies de Half Moon Bay: I have no idea.
Raza de San Jo: No one to think about.
Raza de Hayward: No one to think of.

Pico Rivera Cruising Blvd.
Homies de south side Whittier

On this particular weekend the Pico Rivera cruising boulevard was not happening 'cause the placas closed the boulevard early due

REYNALDO
AND LADIES
DE SAN JOSE

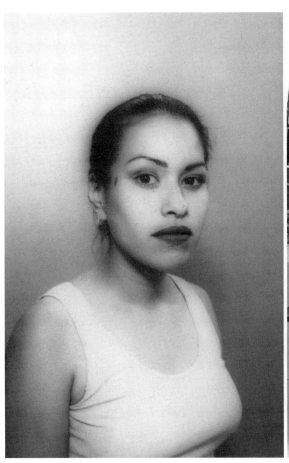

(LEFT TO RIGHT)
REYNA DE SAN JOSE,
RAZA DE SAN JO,
RAZA DE HAYWARD,
LADIES DE HALF MOON BAY

to some pedo that went down the previous weekend. Now, to all the "Brown-n-Proud" gente out there, let's not forget what cruising is all about! It's to have some fun! For hinas to pick up vatos, vatos to pick up hinas and to check out the firme ranflas. If pedo is to go down, then let it be settled in our machismo mannerism, face-to-face. Como los machos que somos!

Young "Brown-n-Proud" de Daly City

MVL: What do you think about 187?

Jackie: It's stupid, because they know this is our land, and that's why they want to kick us out. They think we get welfare and all the homeless are white people. Our people work hard. And they want to kick us out of our land.

Angelina: They should not have 187. Their ancestors came from Europe and Asia.

MVL: Message to La Raza.

Jennifer: Let's try to get our land back. Think before you do something that you might regret.

Carina: Unite and make people get back the land.

Stephanie: Don't fight each other; fight for our rights.

Evelyn and Jackie: Don't be stupid and be in a gang, we need our Raza to get back our land.

Daisy: Think about your Raza first before you do something crazy.

Anielka: Think about our Raza, let's put a stop to this gang fighting and let's get together and do something about our land.

MVL: Girls, thank you for your palabras and for speaking from your corazon. And I know that you girls will bring up our gente in the future. Organize and believe in yourselves and always remain faithful to our cultura! Estas chicas son Mexicanas, Guatemaltecas, Nicoyas y Salvatruchas, La Raza!

(LEFT)
HOMIES DE
SOUTH SIDE
WHITTIER
(RIGHT)
PANCHO DE
SAN PEDRO

MC BOULEVARD

17.

RAZA IN THE MUSIC INDUSTRY

MVL: Ora! Boulevard, what have you been doing since our last interview?

Boulevard: I been performing at the oldie concerts, traveling through the southwest, and I have performed with Malo, Tierra, Zapp and Rogers, One Way, Sly Slick and Wicked.

MVL: Any new releases?

Boulevard: I have two new ones, *Love On My Mind* and the new release of *I Remember You Homie*. I also just did a song with Roger Troutman of Zapp, the new version of "Gangster and the Priest."

MVL: Where could gente get your CD and tape?

Boulevard: Tower Records, Blockbuster Music, Sounds of Music in East LA and Red House.

MVL: For our new readers out there in Aztlanville, how did you get into the music business?

Boulevard: Pues, I took it upon myself to go look for a producer who would listen to my music, and I found one. Then my first demo was created in 1991.

MVL: Hey ese, don't you find it unfair that we, La Raza, are the majority in Califas and throughout the southwest, and yet the DJs on the radio stations don't play our gente's music?

Boulevard: Hell yeah it's unfair, because we have so much talent and we don't get represented. Yet we are the audience and supporters.

MVL: So why do you think Raza musicians don't get exposure on TV and radio stations like other musicians?

Boulevard: One of the reasons is because we don't have the connections to get on the radio and TV. It is limited for Raza.

MVL: How could Raza support our Raza musicians?
Boulevard: Request us on the radio, buy the CDs and tapes (don't dub them) and go to our concerts.

MVL: Do you feel that one day our gente will unite and have a peace treaty throughout Califas?
Boulevard: I think it's possible. I think that one day our future generación will wake up and realize that we should treat each other as carnales y carnalas with respect toward each other.

MVL: What is the mensaje you are giving through your songs?
Aztlan Underground: Awareness of self and truth. We La Raza have been brainwashed since the coming of the whites to these lands. When they conquered the Aztecs, our ancestors were raped, and so we became mestizos—but we are more indigena than white. Science proves it, plus you can see it with your own eyes. Brown skin came from here. So we try to tell Raza the truth about our history and where we came from. Before the whites came, we were in balance with the Earth. Our gente had calendars, medicine; we were an advanced cultura but now we are confused as to who we are. Terms like Hispanic and Latinos are used to confuse la gente. It is a way to remove us of our roots, which are indigena!

MVL: Define indigena for our Linda Raza.
Aztlan Underground: The word indigena means native to the land. White people are not indigena because they are not originally from here. They are from Europe. We, La Raza, are originally from this land. So when the gavas call us wetbacks, they know what they are doing. They are trying to confuse us, the indigena people, as to our conecta to the land. If anyone is a wetback, it is the gavacho because they stole our tierra illegally. This is why we want Raza to know they are indigena, because it will empower us.

MVL: How long have you been in the music business? How did you get started?
Mr. Azteca: I've been in it for two years. I got started while doing tiempo in YA. I was in a lot of talent shows in which I was the only Mexicano among all the blacks. Some Raza supported me, and others did not. Even though some gente did not support me, I went on with my dream, and when I got out I hooked up with MC Boulevard.

We recommend a song called "Perdoname Jefita." Got a lot of positive responses from jefitas/os, gangsters and Veteranos. The song came out of my heart; I wrote it for my jefa.

MVL: Where does your career stand at this time?
Mr. Azteca: Right now I'm working on three songs that are going to be on a compilation with various rap artists. The third song is a Spanish hip-hop verse that's going to be on an MC Boulevard song.

MVL: Any palabras of encouragement to our beloved Raza?
Mr. Azteca: To any Raza out there that have any dreams or goals,

MR. AZTECA
(TOP),
AZTLAN
UNDERGROUND

never let the jealous people's negativity feed your minds. It takes a lot of patience and dedication. You only live once, so you might as well do it and enjoy it.

"Perdoname Jefita" can be found on MC Boulevard's newest release, *I Remember You Homie.*

MVL: Tell my readers a little about yourself, ese.
Moses: I'm Moses Largaespada, born and raised in Los Angeles. I'm a former gang member.
MVL: Ora! So you're a born again vato trying to reach your goals. Firme! Now, what made you change?
Moses: One night I got blasted in front of my jefita, and after seeing her tears, it made me realize that I did not want that life anymore. Plus, I wasn't able to go to any neighborhood without watching my back. Now I'm doing better, 'cause I'm trying to come up in the rap music industry.

MVL: How did you get involved in the rap industry?
Moses: MC Boulevard hooked me up. He's my counselor in my school. He introduced me to a lot of people that gave me an opportunity in recording. My next step is to keep writing my songs and sending them to label companies, and hopefully they will give an opportunity to a young brother.

MVL: Don't give up, and keep on with your goals.

Mundi Dialect is a Latino rap group out of Miami, Florida by three members known as:
> Advikit-1: Puerto Rican from Miami, Florida
> Cyco: Nicaraguense from Daly City, Califas
> Dizzy: Nicaraguense from New Orleans

Here is the story of how three Raza members started making their dream of becoming a successful rap group a reality.

Cyco: We all had our own ambition to rap. When we started we were three different groups in high school back in the early '90s, but the three groups ended up breaking up because of some problems. First myself and Advikit-1 got together, and when Dizzy got back from New Orleans we made him part of the Dialects. So our group

(LEFT)
MUNDI DIALECT,
MIAMI, FLORIDA

(RIGHT)
MOSES LARGAESPADA,
DE LOS ANGELES
WITH MR. AZTECA

is three groups in one.

Advikit-1: After years of doing shows, the independent hip-hop labels in Miami weren't too organized. We decided to learn the business side and ended up incorporating our own independent label, called "Assailant Records," in 1993.

MVL: What is the final goal you want to conquer as a group?

Dizzy: We wanted to be a hit nationwide and also get picked up by a major label. And get recognition as "Nicoya rappers" in the hip-hop industry. Music is and always will be my life.

Advikit-1: Our goal is also to establish a label for other Latino groups to help our Raza not get taken over. No matter how big we get, the doors to our record label will always be open to our Raza brothers.

Cyco: To put out a message in my words that will unite our gente because we are the strongest tribe from South to North America.

Dizzy: We also want to get to know all the firme ladies out there!

MVL: Any last comments?

Mundi Dialect: We are not associated with any other companies, we do our own promotions and distributions. We are doing it for the love of making records, not for the money. We don't have to dress up in shiny suits and dance around to make it. We'll always represent our Hispanic roots in everything we do. Those who want to support us are welcome, and those that don't could just make way for the Mundi Dialect. Ready or not, here we come!

18.

LOW RIDING:
A CHICANO LIFESTYLE

One of the most misunderstood lifestyles is the low rider car club members. But before I get into it, agarren la onda! Low riding is a Chicano lifestyle that was created by the Chicanos to bring unity among La Raza! Back in the days, low rider car clubs would invite car clubs from all over Califaztlan for big family gatherings. Wives and girlfriends would talk about girl things while guys would talk about their cars and how and where they bought and traded certain car parts and so on. They had big family gatherings, but the cops did not respect the Chicano car club members and guests, so they constantly harassed them and kicked them out of their gathering places.

Gente, ask yourself, for how much longer are you going to let marranos kick you out of the parques and further disrespect you and your guests and club members? We are no longer living during the 1800s, when the rangers and sheriffs rushed into our people's homes to kill kids and rape women as the men would die defending them! Nowadays, you have video cameras and hundreds of eyewitnesses. Shit gente, wake the fuck up and sue the pinche marranos and, furthermore, lock 'em up! It's illegal the things they do to us, so why do we let it happen? It really frustrates me, because the low rider Chicanos put a lot of time, money and love into doing things correctly, and here come the pigs harassing them and disrespecting them, and gente should not tolerate this bullshit any longer! Videotape them and get a good mouthpiece (abogado), and shake up that money tree and put them in jail. Network with other low rider car clubs and do something about it, gente. Everybody gets pulled over and harassed. Call the media and do whatever you have to do to stop the cops from disrespecting you. You do not see cops going into white people's gatherings and harassing them! So why are you letting yourself and your camaradas and familia and guests get pushed

(TOP)
OAKLAND'S
POLICE LOW
RIDER CAR

(BELOW LEFT)
OAKLAND'S
FIRE DEPT. LOW
RIDER CAR

(BELOW RIGHT)
DUKE'S CAR
CLUB AND
FRIENDS

around by the marranos when you are simply having a family gathering? I know all the hard work that low rider car club members do and all the positive things they do for the barrios, and I get a little upset when the pigs harass you, homies.

One perfect example of a true role model for the low rider community is Chuie Martinez, the president of Duke's Car Club de Santa Clara. Chuie's chapter has sponsored a lot of fundraising benefits so our gente in different barrios can have a better life. For example, his low rider club raised $3,000 for a little girl's family in Watsonville after she got killed in a drive-by. They sponsored sports events for young "Brown-n-Proud" that are locked up and raised money for a day care center for teen moms in school and so on.

Yet all of these positive things are never mentioned in the media! And hundreds of other low rider car clubs do the same for their communities, but the media don't mention it! There are always some pigs ready to harass them. In addition, low rider car club members pull in the little chavalitos and get them to focus on low rider bike clubs and support them to stay in school. It's a Chicano way of life with a lot of creativity!

Nowadays the Oakland police and fire departments have gotten into the low rider movement by having their own low rider cars. I just hope the Oakland cops spread the word to other departments that low rider clubs are good people that are bettering their communities!

Chuie Martinez, president, Duke's Car Club
(To a great person, Chuie Martinez de Duke's Car Club, Santa Clara. Rest In Peace. You will be missed! But your spirit will be among your loved ones!)

MVL: What's the Duke's Car Club history?
Chuie: It started in 1962 in Los. Now there are 16 chapters and we, Santa Clara County, became the fourth. We are a family oriented car club. There is a three-month probation period, and we look for gente that have familia and some kind of trade.

MVL: What has the Santa Clara chapter done for the community?
Chuie: When a lil' girl from Watson got killed by a drive-by, we put on a benefit car show and raised $3,000 to give to her family. In Santa Cruz

we put on a car show for the Boys and Girls Club. We also work with kids so they can build their low rider bikes, and we take them to our BBQs. We are trying to get kids away from trouble.

MVL: What advice do you have for the young "Brown-n-Proud?"
Chuie: Emphasize education, and if you get kicked out of school, then do home study.

Classic Dreams

MVL: How do car clubs like Classic Dreams C.C. bring our gente together?
Danny (Pres.): In the old days, we fixed up cars and went out with the familias. Now we fix cars to look nice and drive them. We get together with different families. Like you, you're from San Francisco, and you are here with family. All of our families should come together from the Bay Area to Los Angeles so we can give our people a good feeling.

MVL: As a jefito, how do you think las madres y padres could discipline their hijas/os?
Danny: A parent needs to be involved with them and bring them to community events and be a good role model. If you like to drink, then be a social drinker and don't bring it home, or your kids will not respect you. You must do things together as a family, and be there for them.

Ladies de Gilroy

MVL: What do you ladies think of today's event?
Ladies: It's good for people that get into trouble, as it gives them something to do. It's good that no one is maddogging, but some of the guys need to respect the girls.

Majesty Car Club in El Paso, Tejas

MVL: As a car club, what have you done for your community?
Majesty: Back in 1987 we used to do Christmas shows in which to

enter you had to bring a toy that was worth at least ten dollars. Bud and KBNA were our sponsors, but about two years ago a shooting occurred in which a car got hit and we lost our sponsorship. Now we are trying to get a bike show together for Christmas 1996.

MVL: What are some activities to keep the chavalones occupied?
Majesty: A bike club, so they could get involved.

MVL: How do you guys help each other?
Majesty: Our golden rule is to look not at what you ride but at who you are. Our club is a familia. We try to help each other out when someone needs any kind of help.

MVL: How do the placas treat the low rider clubs?
Majesty: They stereotype us as gangs, so they consider car clubs as gangs. We are not a gang, we are a car club trying to live a better life with each other.

MVL: The marranos know that car clubs are not committing any wrongdoing, but they will continue to harass you guys unless you and the other car clubs become a political force to get them off your throats! Do you guys vote?
Majesty: Twenty of us have just registered to vote.

MVL: What's your New Year's resolution?
Majesty: Try and unite the Raza as one, for we are all carnales. We are going to build a coalition with Latin Pride, Royal Aces, Zapata, Slow-n-Low, Oldies, Alliance, Imperials, Cruisers and Presence Car Clubs.

Duke's Car Club Benefit Car Show for Teens With Tots
Mike's 1950 Chevy Troca

Cupertino High School has a day care center for teenage moms so they can get their education. Their chavalitos get taken care of all day while the teenage jefitas attend classes. Duke's and Impalas C.C. threw a car show to raise money for a playground so the little chavalitos could play.

San Francisco Car Show

It was a firme Sunday mid-afternoon. Homie Woody de San Fran Mission and I had a few cold pistos before going into the car show. San Franeros as well as all them firme hinas from all over the Bay Area enjoy themselves, and everybody has their hands full.

MVL: What do you think of the low riding movemiento?
Robert, 53 Chevy de Frisco's Finest CC: I love it! It's the shit, Frisco's Finest. All love to my carnal Steve.
Tomas: It's firme, holmes.
Vanessa: It's the bomb!

South Gate Azalea Park Car Show
MC Pancho and Super Model Dazza.

Mr. MC Pancho, the *Mi Vida Loca* magazine rep for the Harbor Area, covered the firme car show in South Gate Azalea Park. "The Blue Rose" '64 Impala won for best low rider out of 350 cars.

Daly City Jefferson High Car Show
Homie from Nuestro Estilo C.C. hopping his firme ranfla.

Again the gente from Nuestro Estilo Car Club organized a firme car show in the town of Daly City at Jefferson High. Car clubs and gente from all over the Bay Area came to enjoy themselves at this firme happening. Thanks to all the gente from Nuestro Estilo Car Club and the school officials of Jefferson High for letting La Raza enjoy our positive creativity.

MVL: What do you homies think of the car show?
East Side Daly City: The car show is cool. A big shout-out to all the homies from Daly City.
Chuco: I'm glad we are all here kicking it with all the homies without the huras tripping. A shoutout to all the homeboys doing tiempo behind the wall. Keep striving for the betterment of La Raza and keep your heads up.
Ladies: We congratulate all the guys who are hopping their cars.

(TOP)
EVERGREEN
VALLEY CAR SHOW

(BELOW)
DALY CITY
JEFFERSON HIGH
CAR SHOW

Evergreen Valley Car Show in San Jo

MVL: What does the low riding movement mean to you gente?
Sabor Latino: It's cool right now, but it's dying out because of the color bullshit. People don't want to cruise, 'cause they don't want their cars messed up all because you're from another town. We (the car clubs) get a bad rap because of the young chavalos. It's not what it used to be; people used to have respect, and now people throw bottles. Chavalitos don't know how to act to us older vatos, which makes us not go out.

Evergreen Valley Car Show

"No Role Models"
The Evergreen Valley Car Show was at Evergreen Valley College in San Jo, Califaztlan. It was not as full as was anticipated, but there were a lot of firme ranflas, pues ya saben! Pura Raza creativity at its best. So *Mi Vida Loca* asked the "Brown-n-Proud" gente at the car show the following question: "Who is your role model?"

Jose de Inspirations: I don't have a role model, I'm into cars.
Screech de Inspirations: My dad, 'cause he does what he has to do in life, and he is a hard worker.
Chivo: My brother, who taught me how to box.
Manuel: My dad, 'cause I would still be locked up if it wasn't for him. He got me into cars.

Robby de Impalas C.C.: I never really had a role model. Maybe my uncle, who is incarcerated, 'cause he was always there and told me the things to get away from, and taught me from his mistakes. He told me the things to look out for and gave me positive thoughts.
Eddie: My uncle Manuel inspired me to build cars. He passed on the '59 to me and put me on the low rider scene.
Juan: My dad, for he has always been working and always told me that whatever I want, I have to work for it.

Voices de Aztlan—Bike Club in Oaklond

MVL: What is the purpose of your bike club?
Raza: To stay out of trouble.
  – A hobby to have fun.
  – Something to be proud of; it's custom made from our garage.
  – No queremos copiones, esto es solo para La Raza.

MVL: Simon! Like low riding, it's a Raza thing! Nuestro estilo must be exposed! Let's value our ways.
MVL: How do you feel that President Clinton and Governor Pete Wilson are building prisons so that you young and proud chavalones would rot in them?
Raza: Not too good. Que no mamen!
MVL: Pues, think about voting, and when you turn 18, vote against those human vultures. Sometimes you will just vote for

(LEFT)
SAN PANCHO
BIKE CLUB

(BELOW)
EVERGREEN VALLEY
CAR SHOW

the lesser evil; until we get our act together and create our own political party.

A chavalone was jumped by the Africanos and then got suspended. The pedo started over some B.S. that an Africano provoked. *MVL* does not mean to make an enemy out of the Africanos, for the gavacho is enough! When the Africanos were brought here by the gavachos, our ancestors helped the Africanos by giving them a place to kick back in—but they sure have forgotten, just like the gavachos have forgotten. But I'm proud to say that este chavalone stood his ground as a warrior! Carnalito, use your "huevos" to create positive things when you get back to school. Like a Raza club. A club by Raza and for Raza, like your bike club. Go back to school and demand your credits; it's not your fault that cowards attacked you.

San Pancho Bike Club

MVL: Why did you guys organize a low rider bike club?
Stranger: To get fame. People respect you when you do constructive stuff, like this. We do it to show the public what low rider bikes are all about.

MVL: What does San Pancho Bike Club have set up for the future?
Julio: For the future, we just want to have the baddest bikes in San Francisco.

MVL: Are you vatos looking for members?
Klame: We are not really looking for members, but if we see you cruising in a firme low rider bike, whether you are a brown male or female, we just might scoop you up and put you on the team.

– P.S., To all you haters, this is a hobby that takes time, talent, money and respect. So when you see gente with a firme low rider car or bike, don't hate them for it.

BEHIND THE SCENES
OF *MI VIDA LOCA* MAGAZINE

Qvole mi gente, I'm Rey, publishing editor de *Mi Vida Loca* magazine, and I'm going to take you to behind the scenes of an *MVL* interview. Now, my mission was to set up an *MVL* junta with two of my bloodbrothers out in the desert. Why? 'Cause no one had a choice! And this junta was long due. Qvo ese "A" and "F."

Whenever I go deep into the corazon of Southland, 90 percent of the time I take the SFM Blvd. exit in San Fernando Valley, because that's the actíon spot—plus that's where I refuel after that big-ass hill that I hate! De todos modos, the SFM Blvd. exit in San Fer is the ideal spot to know the que pasos in the Valle (to a good perro homie Gibby de San Fer, a big qvo down your way and trucha loco).

Within minutes after making my stop, I ran into some homies del Valle. So I walked up to one of the homies and told him about the revista—then all of his homies got out of their car with a puzzled look, so I carefully went to my bucket to get a few revistas and showed it around. Then about five police cars barricaded us and told us to go against the wall (you gente know the routine, que no!). While the placas were checking and questíoning everybody, I noticed one placa checking out *Mi Vida Loca* magazine. The placas were stating that the spot where we were at was a hot spot, 'cause within the last week there had been three murders. We all got ID'd and questíoned as to why we were there. Then I told a placa that I stopped the homeboys so I could interview them for the magazine, and that it was my fault for them to be at the spot where we were at. Their immediate reactíon was "shut up." So what's a vato to do but stay silent, que no!

Afterwards the other vatos were asked about their reason for being "there." The placas couldn't believe that I was a San Franero,

even after they saw my ID. So I told them that I'm on a business trip for *Mi Vida Loca* magazine, a positive magazine for the Raza. Later, I was told that I could leave, but then I said that I wanted to finish my interview with the homies and that I was the one who flagged them down for an interview. Then the placa restated that what they were doing was nothing personal, it was just that we were in a war zone where three vatos had been gunned down this week, and the week hadn't even ended. So I told them that I understood, and that *MVL* magazine is on the front lines trying to bring out the positive side.

So the placas left, and no one was taken away. Then I told Miguel, the older vato from the group, that we should wrap up the interview. One of the homeboys said, "Follow us to my chante, I live just a few blocks around here."

"Firme, let's do it," I answered.

So I followed one ranfla while the other ranfla was in back of me. Those few blocks seemed hell of long, 'cause it was not around no corner! Ha! Finally we got to a place where we were in front of a parque. Everybody got off their ranflas, and then Miguel and I started talking.

"So what's your magazine all about, dog?" Some of his homies were looking toward us, while the younger ones were just cabuilando.

So I said, "The revista is about us, La Raza. I don't give a shit whether gente are Sureños, Norteños, Maravillosos or Paisas. I interview everybody, and as long as they give me my respect, I'll respect them. And what I like to do with it is to make all of us understand that killing each other for no good reason is stupid as fuck, 'cause while we are trying to kill one another, we have the gringos setting us up for failure in their political, social, economical and

educational arena in our own land. So what's to become of our race if we are killing it off? We don't make any movidas on the gavas, we just prey on our own."

Then Miguel said, "What I'm going to tell you, dog, comes from the heart, and it hurts me. There'll never be peace among our gente, 'cause there are fools that think they are too good, and then we have the younger vatos doing drive-bys, and if someone innocent is on their way—oh well, it's their fault. The youngsters haven't suffered, and they don't have any respect. No one gives a fuck! I've been in the pinta and the carnales teach you respect! Only in the pinta Sureños are united just like Norteños are united in the pinta. Now the only way we could have peace in the calles is if everybody from the pinta comes out at the same time, then we would start respecting each other—but that is not going to happen! So the drive-bys and killings will go on. Some people try to do the right thing, but others fuck it up, 'cause they try to be better. It's just the way it goes. The killings in the Valle will not stop, there's no way of stopping it!"

Then I paused, and we elaborated about reasons that the "Southern United Raza" was not on course. The rest is confidential. Since I had set up an unexpected *MVL* junta out in the desert, I had to go. Then I was invited to come back by a couple of homies.

While driving to my destination, the same words that homie Miguel said have been told to me over and over again by all kinds of vatos. Homeboys from Norte and Sur Califas and homies from Tejas, pero aun I don't give up in trying to reach out to at least a few of the solid vatos out there, 'cause if a solid vato turns to school to better his life and better his family situation, then that vato will carry on the torch to keep our machismo and our cultural way of being alive, away from the influences of the gavas and tintos. Porque nuestras costumbres valen!

HOMIES DE
SAN FERNANDO
VALLEY

POSARENAS
Y HOMIE EN
TIJUANA,
MEXICO

Now as for the madness out there, there's only two curatíon! To go back to our cultural way of being and bring machismo back into the calles! That means not hidden in a speeding car! Not hidden among a group of your homeboys while your rival is greatly outnumbered! I know for a fact that we as vatos can go back to our honorable and cultural ways of machismo. Within our cultura a man of machismo stands on his own two feet, does not rat on his socios, keeps his palabra—for it is a sign of his honor and his dignity—and, for the most part, a hombrio of machismo will contribute to our destiny for the liberatíon of our beautiful Indio-Hispano race, La Raza!

After a few hours on the road, I reached my destinatíon. As always, it was a firme *MVL* junta, in which everything is strictly confidentíal. Then I rushed to the next destinatíon just to find no one to greet me, so I figured I'd conduct the second *MVL* junta the next day. So I headed to the nearest city, which was Calexico, but I decided to hit up Mexicali instead. By the time I got there my brains were "sunburnt," so I went to a hotel. And let me tell you, gente, cold water felt good, but later it got me all sick, and gave me headache and even a stomachache. I woke up early the next day feeling as if a truck had run me over. Regardless, I went to the junta just to find out that it was moved to a different place, so I floored the pedal for about a straight hour and half. Shit, my bucket was another "Speedy Gonzales" out there in UFO country pero le saque la "m..." 'cause it died on me. And to make this shorter, I got stuck in the desert for a few hours! Hours later, a viejito and his perro gave me a ride to Diego Town. From there I found out that my other junta would be postponed to a future date and place. So I took the trolley to Tijuas, drank a couple of pistos and got sick due to those hours in the desert. So I went to crash in one of them $13 hotel rooms, in which the music underneath vibrated my whole room. I got a little mad,

REY AND HOMIES
DE LYNWOOD
AND WATTS,
SOUTHERN
CALIFORNIA

'cause I wanted a restful sleep. Ha! Whoever heard of a restful sleep in Tijuas pero de todos modo I changed my room and dropped dead to sleep. Ha!

The next morning I got up at about four a.m., took a playa and strolled to the "linea," but along the way I heard "Reynaldo!" I looked and it was Posarenas, a vato from 19th St. who now lives in Tijuana. I looked and asked, "Fuck, what happened to you, antes estavas bien Gordito."

"Tu sabes," Posarenas answered back.

After a while, I told them I had to pull descuenta so I could get the Greyhound. Then he said, "Tell my homies from 19th St. that I'll see them soon."

"Tell you what, I'll put it on *MVL* so that they could read it, al rato," I answered.

Upon reaching San Fran, my perro Neto de San Fran Mission gave me a lift to Salas, Watson, San Jo and other places to take care of *MVL* deliveries. Gracias homie. As for my bloodbrothers "A" and "F," ahi nos watchamos carnales.

On one particular night, in a particular city, I was driving my '64 Chevy SS Impala with two vatos; "N" and "G." I've known "G" for quite some years, and he's the type that "plays the part." I know what he is and what he is not. At this time, "N" has been recovering from shotgun wounds and was not in top shape. I recall going into a tienda for some chocolate and some Doritos, leaving "N" and "G" in my ranfla. When I came back from the tienda both vatos were arguing, and "G" had pulled a knife and put it to "N's" neck.

"Hey 'G' what the fuck is wrong with you!? Homie is a cripple and you're fucking with him, you fucking leva." Then I threw my chocolate at him and got him out of my ranfla. He got up and left.

Homie "N" was white as a savana and said, "Gracias Rey, I

owe you." So I made him my rep for my barrio, where kids as young as nine were carrying cuetes. I remember playing with plastic swords at that age!

Months later, we made arrangements for "N" to pick me up at the Greyhound station in Los Angeles. He picked me up with his homegirl. "N" stated that some of his homies were at Lupe's house, his homeboy jefita, 'cause they were investigating an incident with a homeboy.

"He's been accused of... so we're trying to see if it's true or just rumors," stated "N." Then he added, "Rey, tomorrow night we are gonna party with some hinas from Longo."

"That's a trip, 'cause a couple of years ago, I met some hinas from Longo in San Fran, and my homeboy Lucan and I helped them drive back to Longo. We kicked it firme. My hina was firme! She was a schoolteacher for little kids; and damn, holmes, she had some nice nalgotas," I said.

"Hey dog, these hinas aren't schoolteachers, but they look fine. Oh by the way Rey, when we get to the canton we have to rush inside! Our rivals live right across the street and sometimes we blast each other when any of us pass by. But, we always have a homeboy posted to return fire."

When his homegirl dropped us off, we rushed inside the canton. Luckily no "snipers" that night. A few of "N's" homeboys were there talking about the "accused" homie. I was introduced, but I felt awkward 'cause of the situation I walked into about their homeboy "accusation." I was shown to my sofa out in the back, and a few of them started saying how fucked up things were, 'cause everybody was shooting at each other and so everyone was on constant 24 hour alert. Everyone was edgy, but looking forward to the interview and the Longo party.

The next day, everybody was showing up one at a time. Then I heard, "Rey, hit the floor!" "BOOM!" I dropped to the floor and crawled to the living room where everybody was on alert. Then "B" entered with his 9mm in his hand and said, "There's two carloads following me." While "T" was looking outside the window with his cuete and said, "No hay pedo, they just cruised on by." After enough of the homeboys showed up for the "trial," they went on.

At the end, the vato was found innocent because of lack of evidence and no real witness to accuse him. But hardly anyone was talking to him as if he was guilty. I kinda felt sorry for the guy.

"Dispensa dog, but we had to take care of the barrio's business first," "N" told me. "Homeboy is lucky, 'cause if there would have been evidence against him, he would have been thrown out of the barrio, and we never would have acknowledged him again, and he would probably have killed himself 'cause he would have no one. Not even a mother or a father, they were killed long ago. We're all he's got."

Before the interview, "L" showed up all excited, stating that he just popped a few cuetasos to their "enemies," and so the interview had to be done de avolada, for the canton was a perfect target. Then "B" told the homies where to meet later to head down to the Longo party. Afterwards, I asked "B," "How come you vatos don't handle shit a los putasos?"

"It's fucking sad, homeboy, but right now the barrio we're up against, they used to be our little homies at one time," he replied. "When we were chavalitos we all used to play together. Then certain vatos wanted to run shit, and we grew apart. Antes carnal, jugavamás football, we used to have football games when the veteranos were around; now they're all locked up and we're having shooting games. But it's real, homeboys get shot at and some of us die. Our childhood friend shot "N" with a shotgun, and killed a couple of homeboys. What are you supposed to do?"

"You and me know that there are always a caga palo; just like there's a vato with a higher palabra. You need to one day pull him aside and talk to him to see if you vatos could come up with some kind of treaty. But you both have to be strong enough to keep the rest from not breaking it, and it's hard. But the way I see it is if the Japanese and the U.S. came up with a treaty and if the Russians and the U.S. could come up with a treaty, then why not Chicanos among Chicanos? There's got to be someone con muchos huevos for this."

Then someone called him and he said, "I'll see you at the party later, ese."

"B" gathered the homeboys and told them, "On our way to Longo, no one starts any shit; we all need to get there without getting into any bullshit! There'll be some firme hinas and plenty of pisto. We'll hit the cuts one ranfla at a time, and keep you ears and eyes open for the Longo boys."

Later, after a few hours, we all met at the "spot" and cruised seven carloads deep into Longo territory. We drove through some alleys in order to get into the party house, and one carload at a time went inside the canton. At first there were only a couple of hinas, then later more and more came in and they were looking "de aquellas." A few of them left the homeboys with their mouths all watery and mines tambien. Everybody was having a good time, with plenty of dancing and drinking. I was dancing with a firme hina; then all of a sudden "L" said, "Don't you know that we're supposed to hate you?!" Then the music stopped, and every eyeball was on us! So I thought, if I punch this idiot, I'll get the shit kicked out of me and there won't be any more *MVL* representation in this barrio, and I don't have a car. If I pretend not to hear him, then I'll look like a big fucking pussy. Fuck it, I'm going to tell him exactly how I feel, and if they kick my ass, I just hope to be able to walk back to the Greyhound place. So I looked at "L" straight in his eyes and said, "Simon ese! I know that! And I hear it all the fucking time from Sureños and Norteños—but what am I supposed to do, stop my magazine because vatos don't like each other? It's my magazine and I call the shots, and I chose to be down here 'cause I gave my palabra that *MVL* is for all of us! Now ese, would you go all the way to Northland and interview a bunch of crazy Norteños for a magazine that no one gives a fuck about but that has become part of you? Would you do that, ese?!"

Then the homie shook his head, and right away "B" said, "Homie Rey came down here with respect, so we are going to treat him with respect! Orale! On with the party."

The music went back on and people went back to dancing and drinking. Then "B" said to both of us, "No hay pedo, let's just have a good time."

"The homie gots things on his mind," I said. "I think we should go out and have a turica just the two of us."

We all agreed, so homie "L" and I talked about things, things that were beyond our control, then about la vida loca that takes us six feet under. Then we went back inside and had a shot of tequila para "La Vida." Minutes later, homie "D" said, "We're running out of pisto and tequila; who wants to go with me to the tienda?" I volunteered, and so did "L." We were told to be real trucha, 'cause we were in "enemy" territory. When we got to the tienda, I stayed outside as a lookout. I saw a few vatos walking toward me, so I walked in their direction and asked for the tiempo. They responded and asked, "Hey dog, could you do us a paro and buy us some pisto? We don't have an ID and they card us here."

"Yeah, I'll do it for a pisto," I answered. I went in, told the homies about it and to wait, plus I had the other vatos wait for me around the corner. I gave the vatos their pisto, then I took mine and one of them gave me $5. After they walked away, we all left back to the party. Then I joined the table where gente were playing quarters and, man oh man, I got fuckkked up!

Next day, I woke up with a mean hangover from mixing my drinks. The homies organized a viaje and we ended up having a firme time. A couple of days later, I got dropped off at the Greyhound station and went back home. Just another behind the scenes at *Mi Vida Loca* magazine.

20.

EN MEMORIA DE TUN TUN DE TIERRA BLANCA, SINALOA, MEXICO

I'm writing this behind the scenes in memory of "T-T." But before I start, just a reminder that my jale with the magazine was to go to every barrio in Aztlan and plant a seed of hope, motivation, education and positivity to the locos y locas that were trying to kill each other without me sacrificing honor and keeping myself from getting killed.

This behind the scenes story covers a few cities and a lot of people's names, which I will leave out bueno pues!

I was walking in the barrio and a homie I knew was riding shotgun in a firme Mustang convertible. They pulled over and asked me to join them to go partying in another town. I hop on and we made a quick stop to buy some pisto and drove to our destination. We were having a good time cracking up on some jokes and drinking a few cold ones. When we reached our destination, there was a lot to do, for it was a tourist attraction and there were a lot of good-looking hinas, and the older homie was pulling in all kinds of hinas. We got a few directas to their hotel rooms, and man oh man, we were rolling them in like bees in honey, and we were loving it. Until we decided to stock up on the pisto and some liquor for the hotel fandango with the babydolls. Upon our way to the liquor store, we went through a barrio that were known to jump on other vatos disrespecting their familias y todo, though we didn't know that at the time. I noticed a couple of vatos sizing us up, so I walked to them and asked them the way to the tienda, which they gave. Minutes later, they demanded that my homie take off his shirt, then the older homie was telling them that we weren't there to 'cause any problems, we just wanted some pisto, but they demanded that the other homie take off his shirt. By this time, I was pissed, 'cause the homie we were with didn't say a damn thing and was about to take his shirt off. Then, all of the sudden, a group of 15 to 20 vatos came rushing in with sticks and bricks, so I grabbed one of them by the shirt and let him have a few putasos. Then they all rushed me to the ground while I was holding someone's neck, but eventually I let go to defend myself from the putasos, putadas and a brick that was thrown at me. I didn't know at the time that both of the vatos I was with ran away while I stayed. Suddenly, they all ran away—I was being pulled, and I started swinging again. Then, I heard "It's me, homie."

Later I woke up in the hospital, and right away I thought, "Oh no, not another stabbing (#15!)—God, how many more?" But it was only a slice and a couple of bruises, so I was lucky. A cop came in asking me some questions, and I told him that I didn't know anything and that I wanted to be left alone. Then he said that he had some guys detained. I retold him that I didn't know nothing and to leave me alone. Even though they started their shit, there's honor among us Raza that are against our own self-destruction. I even told the nurse not to let the cop come in and bother me. Luckily I left that evening, and the homies drove me back home. Naturally I was pissed off at three things: them putos that jumped me and spoiled my good time, the two so-called homies who left me to fight alone, and missing out on the babydolls that were waiting for us in their hotel room! Ooouch!

Back to the canton, I was arguing with the fellows for running out, and they were telling me that they thought I would run away tambien. My answer was that I would walk away if honor was not sacrificed, but I would never run! I carried a grudge with that barrio mainly because I was no longer a vato that claimed a barrio. I was myself, and I respected those that respected me, and deep down inside I knew I would go back to that same barrio.

About a year later, I ran into a few vatos that were close to that barrio that trashed me on the ground. I explained my situation and told them that all I wanted to do was to go straight putasos with those that were involved. Them vatos were respected by that barrio, and we were firme, so we drove there. They trusted me, and I had to trust them for that particular gesture. So I waited while they talked to the vatos from that hood. About half an hour later, word got out that I was there to throw chingasos with those that fucked me up that night, and that I wanted one-on-one putasos. To my surprise, no one wanted any shit, and they apologized for the pedo. So things got squashed! During this time, there were a few homegirls from a far-away city that belonged to a well known barrio in their part of the woods, and wanted me to go interview them for their barrio. They told me that they would provide me with a place to stay and would make sure no one started any beef with me. We exchanged numbers and I left with the homies.

A couple of months later, I was conducting interviews at those homegirls' barrio. I was lost, so they sent someone to escort me into their barrio. People were partying when I got there, and I felt a little uncomfortable, 'cause I wanted to conduct interviews with everybody having a clear head. So I decided to do interviews the next day instead. Meanwhile, I was offered the chance to drink up, but I passed it up 'cause I have indigenous blood and I get stir crazy sometimes with that firewater. After talking to a few of their homeboys and after talking to the shotcaller, I relaxed a little and accepted a few drinks. Only three drinks, 'cause I'm a light drinker and I was there representing *Mi Vida Loca* magazine. Out of the blue, a vato did not like the fact that I was wearing a red slingshot, so I looked at him and said, "You know what, dog, this red slingshot is gonna stay on me all night, but tomorrow after I take a playa I have to wear a clean one. If you want to buy me a new blue slingshot I'll wear it, 'cause I don't trip on this color bullshit! Sometimes I wear red and sometimes I wear blue. And I'm being told to be careful pero sinceramente a mi me vale. As long as there's respect, then everything is firme." The vato looked at me all crazy and said, "Estas cabron huey" and invited me to a drink. Just my luck, it was tequila, so I told homie that if I drink tequila I would throw up all over and I did not want to do that. But in reality, tequila is a powerful firewater that controls my behavior. Homie respected that and so he offered me some nachos, which I ate all of. Next day, in the afternoon, I conducted the interviews and I gave them my palabra that I would come back personally to show them their interview.

Three months later, I set up a junta so that their barrio would see their interview and to seek out tiendas to sell the revistas. The homegirls told me to be careful, 'cause there'd been a few killings with different rivals, and everybody was on their toes and ready to blast. Upon reaching their city I found myself lost, again! I recognized their side of the city and some streets I remembered—but, just my luck, I left the homegirls' number at home, so I was cruising through the unknown. Then I noticed a couple of vatos standing at a housing complex that seemed like the one I stayed in, and in the back of my mind I remembered what homegirl had told me. I stuck my arm outside and said, "Hey homie, I'm gonna pull a U-turn, so don't trip, I'm looking for..." So I made a U-turn, but not too slow and not too fast, 'cause I didn't want anyone to start blasting thinking I was a rival. When I parked my ranfla, I noticed that I had revistas to show but they were inside the trunk, and said, "Hey homie, I'm Reynaldo de *Mi Vida Loca* magazine, but I got 'em inside the trunk, so don't trip 'cause I'll be getting some magazines." By this point, the vato had a cuete pointed right at me. So I slowly opened the trunk and pulled out some revistas with one hand and placed them on my chest while walking up to the vato and his cuete. Then he said, "Where you from?"

"I told you, I'm from *Mi Vida Loca* magazine," I answered.

"Never heard of it! Where you from ese?" Then I realized I was in the wrong barrio.

He asked me a direct question that needed a direct answer, so I told him, "I'm from San Francisco, and I'm here by myself conducting my jale, which is this here revista which is for everybody. A few months ago I interviewed the gente de "LV" and I gave my palabra that I would be back to show them the revista. Check it out." I offered one.

The vato called his homies, and two more came out while he looked over the revista, and then he said, "You got gangas from all over." "Since you put 'LV' on there, could you put our barrio?" Man oh man was I relieved.

"Simon," I answered.

"My barrio is not as big as 'LV,' but we got some crazy homies in it. How did you get hooked up with 'LV?'"

Then I answered, "That's personal, homie, and I don't talk about another barrio with a different barrio out of respect. All I can tell you is that I'm looking for them to let them know that they're in *MVL* magazine."

"'LV' is well respected out here, as well as hated. My barrio is small and we kind of get along with them, but we want to come out too," he said. "Yo soy 'T-T' and these are my homeboys." We shook hands and then T-T gave me a pisto.

"After we talk for a while, con todo respecto T-T, I have to be on my way so I can find 'LV.'"

"Don't trip, ese, we'll take you there. Let's go to the tienda and I'll buy some more pisto. I like talking to you. I never met a vato de San Fran; shit, holmes, I never been out of here, and your revista is firme."

So we all walked to the tienda, and after leaving the tienda a ranfla pulled over and said, "Aren't you Rey de *MVL*?"

"Simon," I answered.

Then two vatos got out of the ranfla and shook the other vato's hand while the other came up to me and said, "I'm here to take you to the homies, we're all partying at a homegirl's house outside the barrio."

I walked with him away from T-T and his homies, and said "If your barrio gets along with T-T and his gente, is it OK if they come with us, 'cause they greeted me firme?"

"No hay pedo," he answered.

I asked T-T if he wanted to come, and he said, "Fuck yea, I heard 'LV' are crazy and I heard that they throw good ass parties."

I pulled him aside and told T-T that his cuete and any other cuete stays inside the trunk and that they were going under my wing since I'm inviting them. He agreed, and his homies left and only one came with us.

Upon arriving at the "LV" party, the homegirls greeted me and offered some comida and pisto. T-T and his homie were greeted tambien. I had two plates full of carne asada with some homemade salsa con tortillas y Tecate. Man oh man was I hungry! Everybody was happy with the entire revista, while some of them were telling me the latest que pasos, sad crazy shit that locos do. We stayed a couple of hours, and T-T kept on telling me that he and his barrio wanted to be in the revista and that he would take me to the tiendas tomorrow and show me around the city and to a flea market. So I agreed, and he offered his canton for me to stay in. So we kicked it a little more and were invited to come back. On the way to T-T's canton we got pulled over by the cops. They put on their high beams and told us to come out with our hands on the tops of our heads and to kneel on the floor. One cop started searching inside the ranfla and I told him that I didn't want him to look inside my ranfla. They asked if I had anything to hide. So I said, "OK, you can look under the seats, but be careful with the rat poison." They didn't like what I said and commanded me to open my trunk.

"You have no search warrant, first of all, and you guys stop me just because we are homeboys, because of my '64 Chevy, which is a classic?" I said. "Are we living in Nazi Germany? I'm a Jew for you Nazis to kill, or is it because I'm 'Brown-n-Proud' and you're pale faces going after the natives?" Then they really got pissed off.

I was surprised that they didn't start calling for backup to kick our asses while they had guns pointed at us. Surprisingly enough, one "Deputy Dog" stated to just open my trunk and that everything would be OK, or they would tow it to the nearest cop station.

"Look, officers, I don't have the key to the trunk," I said; this time the revistas were in the back seat. "I'm simply out here conducting interviews for a Chicano magazine. I'm Reynaldo and I'm a reporter and the editor of *Mi Vida Loca* magazine, and the fellows are my helpers. If you let me show you a magazine you'll see that I'm legit." The pig looked at the magazine and complained that it was gang-glamorizing, so I said, "You are not looking at it and reading the questions, I'm addressing peace and promoting education! I'm not a Sunday school teacher, and I'm not dealing with altar boys, so my questions and their answers are real! Now, if you insist in breaking into my trunk without a warrant, I'll get my company's lawyer to sue you, and I'll get together groups that protect citizen rights that have been abused. It's your call, officer." They gave me a so-called "fix up" ticket, them fucking pigs. T-T and his homie were happy at the ending, 'cause, after all, T-T's cuete was inside the trunk. Then I explained to T-T that "no matter what we as homies do, whether we are walking, standing or just sitting in front of our own house the fucking marranos are always going to fuck with us. We are so fucking stupid in trying to kill each other that they just sit back and laugh and then they lock up the guys who remain alive. Furthermore, La Raza could avoid all this gun shit, by going back to our old ways, which are the right ways, and eventually we will start respecting ourselves and each other." Then I talked to him about our people's history before the gavachos and after the gavas. Man, I fell asleep on his couch giving T-T clecha on our beautiful Raza.

The next day, T-T thanked me for all the knowledge I gave him, and he showed me around his barrio and took me to some tiendas to sell *MVL* magazine. Then he invited me to some menudo. Later, we went to a flea market, where he introduced me to gente he knew. We found out that his homies were rounded up by the placa due to some pedo. Upon nightfall, I headed back home and T-T kept in touch.

After a few months had passed by, T-T was anxious for me to do an interview, but I was over my head with work and personal affairs. Then one day I called his house, and to my surprise, his number was disconnected. While doing *MVL* business in his city, I noticed a hina with a big shapely butt, estaba puro onions! I couldn't resist, and I went to talk to her. She told me that her homeboy had gotten shot in the back and she needed a ride to the funeral place. I didn't ask any questions, 'cause her nalgas had me hypnotized.

"Where do you want me to take you?" I said.

We went to the funeral place and no one was there. She walked to the coffin and started crying. I got close to her and looked in the coffin and saw my homie T-T inside the coffin! I got this weird feeling and explained to the homegirl that I had met T-T a few months ago and that we got along firme. I told her about my jale and she started tripping about the whole thing 'cause T-T had talked about me and was expecting me. Then she hugged me. She asked me if I could pick up a homegirl that T-T was goo-goo over. We went to pick her up but she wanted a few shots of tequila before seeing T-T, so we went to the tienda and got a botella. We drove someplace and drank it. Homegirls downed that bad boy like water! Then we went back to the funeral place and, to our surprise, T-T's homeboys were all over the place. As we walked, they were all giving me hard looks. I knew something was going to go down, so I expected the worst and hoped for the best. As we walked outside, I noticed the vatos were staring hard, and I was staring hard tambien. I heard, "Rey! Qvo homie!" I turned, and it was four of the "LV" homegirls. They were paying their respect to homie T-T. So we started talking. Then one guy cut into our turica and I gave him a dirty look. Another vato said, "why are you dogging my homeboy for ese?" I turned, and the guy who cut in punched me in the side. I turned to hit him and he went down. Then cuetes were pointed at me and the "LV" homegirls stood by my side and stated that I was OK.

"I came here to pay respect to T-T 'cause we got along firme."

"You paid your respect, now leave," said the guy who punched me, and he hit me again, but I couldn't hit him back because I had cuetes on me.

"If you want to fight, I'll fight you one-on-one, but away from here," I said. "Just you and me, ese." Then a big-ass vato came to me and pulled off his shirt and brandished his cuete and said, "You want pedo ese, you'll fight with this," while pointing to his cuete.

"You have a choice, leave now or fight us as we are," he said.

I felt humiliated (since I had no cuetes 'cause I walk a warrior path and battle mano-a-mano, not like a scared puto).

"I can't fight with guns, so I will leave," I said.

The "LV" homegirls said dispensa, and I walked to my ranfla thinking I might get shot in the back. Feeling like a worthless piece of shit I got inside my ranfla, placed my hands on top of the steering wheel and drove out.

For weeks I couldn't sleep 'cause I didn't get a chance to fight and was humiliated. I would rather get an ass-kicking than feel humiliated. Why was I humiliated? 'Cause I didn't do nothing. I was helpless, and so I had to gain back my self-respect, and so I decided to go back.

I went in search of them with all guts and my bare fists, the one who punched me and the big one that gave me those two fucked-up choices. I waited in a blind spot in their barrio until I saw one of his homeboys. Finally, I grabbed one and scared the shit out of him. I demanded the whereabouts of them other guys. I left palabra on where I would be and for them to see me there. Word came back to me saying that a few of them didn't agree with the pedo. I left, told my blood brothers about it, and got clecha on all that I was risking over some chavalas. Like everybody else, I'm not perfect, only the Creator is. And like any other human I make mistakes. But I had no cuetes, solomis manos!

Rest in peace T-T, dispensa for my delay. To Tun Tun de Tierra Blanca, Sinaloa, Mexico ¡Tierra de Raza Pesada!

21.
MURALES

From Norte Califaztlan to Sur Califaztlan and all the way to Chuco Tejaztlan,
I present estos firme murales.

SAN FRAN MISSION DISTRICT

(THIS PAGE)
DECOTO

(OPPOSITE
PAGE, TOP)
BIG HAZARD,
LOS ANGELES

(OPPOSITE
PAGE, BOTTOM)
BARRIO LIL' VALLEY,
LOS ANGELES

(THIS PAGE),
SAN FRANCISCO
MISSION DISTRICT

(OPPOSITE PAGE,
TOP) ARIZONA
MARAVILLA, EAST
LOS ANGELES

(OPPOSITE PAGE,
BOTTOM) BARRIO
NUEVA ESTRADA,
LOS ANGELES

(TOP)
CHE,
EAST LOS ANGELES

(BOTTOM)
WHITE FENCE,
LOS ANGELES

22.
A WORD FROM OUR SPONSORS:
MI VIDA LOCA ADVERTISERS

Doré
STUDIO   AUDREY REVELL
(415) 282-3321
2442 Mission Street, San Francisco, CA 94110

Dr. Aris Carcamo
optometrist

Eye exams

glasses

Contact lenses

2490 Mission St.
San Francisco,
Ca. 94110
(415) 550-8770

307 Grand Ave.
S. San Francisco,
Ca. 94080
415 558-6157

ALSO FROM FERAL HOUSE ⨍ℎ

MUERTE!
Death in Mexican Popular Culture
Edited by Harvey Bennett Stafford
    Contributions from Diego Rivera, José Posada,
    Cuauhtémoc Medina and Lorna Scott Fox
Muerte! explores blood-obsessed multimillion-copy-selling
Mexican publications like *Alarma!* and their
modus operandi. Features never-before-seen photos
by tabloid photographers.
10 x 8 • 108 pages • extremely graphic color photos • ISBN:
0-922915-59-8 • $16.95
Now Available

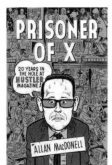

PRISONER OF X
20 Years in the Hole at Hustler Magazine
Allan MacDonell
"*Prisoner of X* is destined to become an American classic
— R. Crumb crossed with William S. Burroughs and the
satiric outrage of Hunter S. Thompson." — Evan Wright,
author of *Generation Kill*
6 x 9 • 314 pages • ISBN: 1-932595-13-9 • $16.95
Now Available

Available Spring, 2007!

MEXICAN PULP ART
The Lurid Supernatural "Historietas"
Introduction by Maria Cristina O'Brien
Here are the amazing paintings by forgotten masters of
supernatural pop art for the covers of '60s pulp novels
and cartoons.
6 x 9 • 140 pages • ISBN: 1-932595-22-8 • full color • $16

TO ORDER FROM FERAL HOUSE:
Individuals: Send check or money order to Feral House, P.O. Box 39910, Los Angeles,
CA 90039. For credit card orders: call (800) 967-7885 or fax your info to (323) 666-3330.
CA residents please add 8.25% sales tax. U.S. shipping: add $4.50 for first item, $2 each
additional item. Shipping to Canada and Mexico: add $9 for first item, $2 each additional
item. Other countries: add $11 for first item, $9 each additional item. Non-U.S. origi-
nated orders must include international money order or check for U.S. funds drawn on a
U.S. bank, or PayPal funds to info@feralhouse.com. We are sorry, but we cannot process
non-U.S. credit cards.

www.feralhouse.com